# WOMEN AND COMPUTING

**Rose Deakin** used to be a full-time professional social worker, subsequently working part time in social research. But in 1981 she made a complete change by going to work for a computer microsystems company, a career she has successfully continued. It was because of her three children that Rose Deakin first became involved in computing. The difficulties and benefits she experienced in learning how to use computers were such that she wanted to pass on her experiences to other women and, she hopes, men.

# WOMEN AND COMPUTING

## The Golden Opportunity

ROSE DEAKIN

MACMILLAN

Series consultant: Ray Hammond

ISBN 0 333 37493 2

First published 1984 by
PAPERMAC
a division of Macmillan Publishers Limited
4 Little Essex Street London WC2R 3LF
and Basingstoke

Associated companies in Auckland, Delhi, Dublin, Gaborone, Hamburg, Harare, Hong Kong, Johannesburg, Kuala Lumpur, Lagos, Manzini, Melbourne, Mexico City, Nairobi, New York, Singapore and Tokyo

Typeset by Bookworm Typesetting
Printed in Great Britain by the Pitman Press, Bath

*For my mother and father, neither of whom know one end of a computer from another but whose encouragement, both moral and financial, has helped their two daughters to take up careers in computing.*

## Contents

*Preface*                                                                          xi

**Part I        The Argument**

Chapter 1   Computing is an Opportunity for Women          15

Chapter 2   Women are not Taking to Computing: the Evidence   21

Chapter 3   Suggested Remedies                                        33

Chapter 4   Future Patterns                                          41

**Part II       Some Ideas and Practical Examples**

Introduction                                                          53

Chapter 5   Possible Applications for the Micro at Home (1)   55

Chapter 6   Possible Applications for the Micro at Home (2)   63

Chapter 7   Nora, Drusilla and Kate                              73

Chapter 8   Rose, Sarah and Mary                                 85

Chapter 9   Christine and Marjorie                               95

Chapter 10  Points Arising from these Examples               101

**Part III      Practical Measures**

Chapter 11  Learning the Lingo                                  107

Chapter 12  Suitable Equipment                                  115

Chapter 13  Getting Started: Training                           123

Chapter 14  Conclusion                                          129

*Notes on the Text*                                                  131

*Glossary*                                                          133

*Index*                                                             145

# Preface

In writing this book I want to point out the opportunities that computers offer to my fellow women, especially at the moment. I want to help them to take in the flood this tide in their affairs which can lead on to such fortune. I want to help men to release what one of their own number has described as 'half the talent' available in the workforce, and so to increase the productivity and success of British firms competing both at home and abroad. Women are not merely a numerically large part of the workforce: they are also a significant part. What is the mighty concept of the electronic office likely to come to if women do not learn to use the new office equipment?

I think it is important at this stage to state my position. Although I am not an ardent feminist – I am too lazy, and perhaps too lacking in principles, to fight the battles of my more vulnerable sisters – I am nonetheless in sympathy with the women's movement. As with all pressure groups, they sometimes give the argument to the other side by their extremism and passion, but it is still important that there are women who are willing to fight this battle, publicize their cause and gradually influence public attitudes for the good.

In this book, however, I am not interested in the rights and wrongs of the feminist cause, or in apportioning blame. I am interested in the position of women in relation to computing and in what can be done about it. If I try to trace causes it is because it is important to look for areas of behaviour and understanding that can be affected or altered immediately or by identifiable practical means. I am concerned neither with reforms that will take generations to produce radical changes, nor with changes that concern wider social attitudes. My interest is in issues that may help women to measure up to the challenge of computing – and especially microcomputing – and get the best possible benefit from it.

What are my qualifications for writing such a book? I am a woman, I have come to computing by an unorthodox route and I have been reasonably successful at it. I cannot, however, claim to have had any kind of struggle along the way, other than with my own lack of knowledge and understanding of the subject. Nor have I ever been thwarted or opposed by men. Rather the reverse: I have felt that my path has been particularly smooth partly *because* I am a woman. I have had more help from the men whom I have encountered in the field of computing than I could have expected, I have experienced no rivalry or jostling for position, and, moreover, I have enjoyed a certain celebrity and freak notoriety just because I am a woman: I am praised not because I do it well, but because I do it at all. This may not be admirable but it is certainly useful.

It has been curious, at the same time, to find myself almost unable to forget that I am female and, therefore, different from most of my professional colleagues, which was not the case in the first half of my working life when I pursued careers more conventional to women. I have been drawn unwittingly into a position where I have watched how the few other women in my field behaved, noticed the way in which they made use of their gender or, more openly, their sex, and have begun to observe myself in the same way.

Two months before I got my first paid job in microcomputing I wrote an article for *Practical Computing* describing the difficulties and traumas of my first nine months. This was held over for publication in a special women's issue and my first feeling on being told this was annoyance that women should be made a special case. The editor understood my reaction and said that he did not like to treat women so, but that in practice it was necessary. It was really the fault of women themselves, he said, as they simply would not take any interest in computing as it was usually presented. Nowadays I find myself agreeing with him and feel impatient with my sex. It is unfortunate that many subjects, and especially computing, quickly develop a flavour that appeals more to men than to women, but this does not happen by design. In something like computing the influences are predominantly commercial: advertising and presentation are geared up to those who respond and who fork out the cash to keep the manufacturers going. Only when times are hard, or they are looking for new markets into which to expand, do the sellers and manufacturers focus on women. At the educational level it is different. Those responsible for educating the nation's children and future workforce should strive to counteract the trend to make computing a male-dominated subject because it is in the country's future interests that all its workers should understand and make use of the new technology.

For these reasons, I have charted my own progress and noted more particularly than I otherwise might have done which aspects were made harder by my being female and which easier. Most of the scoring was on the credit side, and though there have been occasions when men's assumption that any female is present in a menial capacity has been irritating, I have never felt that it handicapped me in any serious way.

In fact, it more often seems to handicap the men themselves, as it either puts them in a false position or makes them unable to get the best out of the women working for them. So as well as writing for women, to urge them to throw off their chains of dependency and grasp the nettle of computing with strength and confidence, I am also writing for men, to urge them to beware lest they fail to utilize their workforce properly and thus fall behind in the great productivity race.

The difficulty lies in how to get through to men. When I mentioned to even the enlightened and intelligent men of my acquaintance that I was writing a book on women and computing I was invariably greeted with a belly laugh and the question, 'Who do you imagine would want to read such a book?' I do not know who would *want* to, but I do know who needs to and who should – and they are not all female.

When faced with the task of learning to use the new technology women labour not only under the technical difficulties, but also under the automatic assumption of men that they are incapable of understanding it. I know several men with first-class degrees and positions of considerable standing who will not attempt to learn about computers even conceptually, let alone in practice, on the grounds that they themselves are completely impractical and unmechanically minded. They, however, are not stereotyped and made to feel foolish because of this. On the contrary, companies take a lot of trouble to set up courses with face-saving titles and carefully worked-out content in order to try to educate senior management (usually male) and so overcome the difficulties that are being experienced when junior staff can run rings around executives, decision-makers, and, worse, signers of cheques.

In an attempt to add substance to some of these arguments, I shall look first at the special benefits that exist for women in computing and then in some detail at the ways in which the arrival of microcomputers can be a heaven-sent opportunity for them. I shall discuss the thesis that women are failing to take to computing and try to see whether there is anything in either the nature of women or the role that they play in modern life that contributes to this. Next, I shall examine whether the problem is in any way exacerbated by the nature and attitudes of men, and explore some possible cures and also some prophylactic treatments.

The second part of the book presents some case studies of women who have made interesting or profitable use of computers, followed by a discussion of possible future trends in social organization and patterns of work. Finally, I have compiled an introduction to the basic ideas and jargon of computing, together with some suggestions for how to get started. Although the material in this last section is duplicated in other literature, I have included it here to give some starting information to those whom, I hope, the rest of the book may inspire to take the first steps.

*Part I*

# The Argument

*Chapter 1*

# Computing is an Opportunity for Women

The argument that microcomputers offer a golden, and perhaps unprecedented, opportunity to women has to be substantiated. In order to do this let us look both at the ingredients that need to be present before one can say that any job is ideally suited to women in general and then try to show that many of these are present in microcomputing in quantities that should start a gold rush for those women with vision and self-interest.

## Characteristics of work traditionally done by women

*Home based*
Let us look first at jobs that have traditionally been done by women. There are all the jobs – or perhaps roles, as they are usually unpaid – that involve running the home and caring for and bringing up children. It may be that there is something particular about these tasks that makes them in themselves attractive and suitable to women, but it is more likely that it is the circumstances of the work that make it ideally 'women's work'. The key circumstance is that it can be done from within the home and this links with the biological fact that women are the bearers of children and thus, as a group, are both physically and emotionally more tied to the home than men – even given the premise that men could mind the home and bring up the children just as well as women. In many ways we are finding that the

traditional home-based methods of feeding babies, of cooking food, of cultivating fields or of designing houses had some built-in logic, so it is perhaps reasonable to assume that there is also some practical logic that explains the closer ties most women feel to the actual place, as well as the conceptual bond of the home.

In 1981, at least 86 per cent of women aged from thirty-five to forty-four had children and these children were still living in the household. Of these women, 79 per cent had children who were currently dependent and 62 per cent were in paid work (20 per cent full time and 42 per cent part time). If the rate of mothers working is divided according to the age of the child, figures show that 70 per cent of mothers with school-age children over ten but only 25 per cent of those with children under five had work.[1] This indicates that women are likely to stay at home to look after small children and it is known that they usually return to work to a lower-status position.

The pattern may be changing for younger women, though even mothers who manage to arrange support services – nannies, child-minders and crèches – are expected to have one eye on the home and more risk of having to stay off work to sort out an emergency. Not many men applying for jobs such as teaching are asked what they would do if their children were ill, whereas for women this is quite common. For such a woman any employment that allows her to work from home and to keep irregular or short hours – 'flexi-time' and 'flexi-place' – has advantages. Microcomputing offers just such opportunities, as I shall discuss later, and, moreover, they are advantages which can be described, in the jargon of the trade, as 'upgradable'. Unlike many kinds of home work, which tend to be low skilled and low status, and which offer no kind of job path or hierarchy, computing skills developed on a part-time basis at home are readily transferrable and can help in careers in the same or related fields at a later date.

*The caring professions: skills of communication*

Looking further than home-based jobs into the world of paid employment, there is a preponderance of women to be found in jobs like teaching, child-care and the caring professions generally. In some cases, like teaching, this may be for a mixture of reasons. The work pattern fits in well with the mothering pattern, and is useful both to mothers seeking work and to women who do not yet have children but who think that they may one day be in that position. The same argument cannot be applied to child-care and some other professional jobs, but it reappears for certain kinds of semi- and unskilled work in factories and assembly lines, where part-time and shift work can be made to fit in with the timetable of maternal obligations.

Women are, of course, drawn to the caring professions for reasons other than convenience. Certain characteristics – the ability to communicate, an interest in the personal details of other human lives, an ability to give emotional support to individuals and work without clear signs of success –

seem to be found more often in women than in men and make them more likely to find satisfaction in these fields. Some of these qualities are invaluable in the field of microcomputing and support the argument that it is an area in which women can succeed because they have something special to offer: not just because they can do anything men can do, but because they can do some things better. The fabric of life is enriched if we can think in terms not only of equal opportunity or equal contribution, but also of equal merit from varied contributions.

At this stage in the development of computing and the automation of traditional processes there is a very great need for education, advice, the translation and communication of new ideas and the provision of intelligible information about this new and awesome information technology. Here the qualities that have always made women good teachers, social workers, interviewers, journalists and supports about the house can be put to good use.

This view is echoed in several articles that have appeared in newspapers and magazines lately. Jan Zimmerman, in *Interface Age,** says that women seem to be not only more able, but also more willing, to make computers 'user-friendly'. She adds that most men are totally unconcerned about documenting systems for the people who have to use them. One of her interviewees added:

> It even extends to training. The other women and I are like mothers; we'll hold their hands, try anything to make the customer feel that the machine is less intimidating. I can't imagine guys doing that... Women are good at listening and explaining. We've been taught by our mothers to be gentle, without needing to prove we're better or that other people are stupid.

Social work, for example, is a field in which it is vital to learn to listen, both to words and to signs (what used to be called non-verbal communication), and the prime aim is to help people to find ways of sorting out their problems themselves. To do this the social worker must be able to identify the problems, and more particularly the causes, and then, with a mixture of leading and stimulating, inspire sufficient confidence and motivation in the client to enable him or her to take some positive and effective action.

Exactly the same skills are invaluable to the computer sales consultant. The people currently discovering and purchasing business 'desk-top' micro-computers tend to have grown up without any grounding in the concepts and techniques of using them. Almost by definition they are people who are successful in their own walk of life, since micros of this kind are not really cheap, and they are used to ordering others around and getting things done for them. Now they are faced with going into a showroom, exposing their ignorance and then going along a painful learning curve. They are not clear quite what the problems are that they wish the computer to solve, but they

*December 1983

recognize that they are at a disadvantage without one. The sales interview or consultancy session follows much the same pattern as a social-work interview. First, set your client at ease and help him relax; next, get him to tell you the problem as he sees it; then help him analyse it and see whether further light can be shed. Then think very fast and see whether you can present him with a plan and some options. Take him through them and make him make the decision, both because he will have more confidence in it that way and also because in the time available you almost certainly will not have been given sufficient information on which to base clear advice. This is a bit more directive than social work, as the customer is asking voluntarily for advice and has indicated his desire to buy something if he can find the right product, but, just as in social work, the ability of women to communicate more easily than many men gives them a clear advantage as sales consultants.

Knowledge of the world and the things that clients are likely to want, the problems that they are likely to be facing, is another advantage. This is not related to sex, but it is to age. Most men in computing, though they may be brilliant at their jobs, are very young and inexperienced in other ways. There is not much opportunity for older men to down tools and change professions, but many women are making a middle-aged comeback after a period of child-bearing, and they have a very special contribution to make if they can gather together enough computing skills to make their employment viable.

These characteristics are important at every level of computing. They are relevant at the professional and programming level to make sure that programs match requirements; at the level of consultancy and analysis; in journalism and the documentation of computers and programs; especially in the area of sales and customer support; and, finally, in training and teaching about computers and programs and the particular application of computer and program to the problem in hand.

### Work requiring systematic and logical approach: office work

Another important area of work for women is the office and all forms of clerical work. Women are often considered to be less systematic than men, and certainly less logical. It is difficult to define exactly what we mean by 'logical', but much work done by women in offices up and down the country is essentially systematic. Even the lowest grade of clerical worker, or a junior typist in a pool, has to be neat, orderly and systematic. An administrative secretary has to be logical above all and her work depends on an efficient system. These qualities are also crucial in computing, and explains why women are already successful at operating, programming and systems analysis, and are to be found at all levels of the mainframe, traditional computer world.

The problem of getting women to involve themselves in subjects like computing is not a serious one at the established professional level of computer programming and in activities involving mainframe and minicomputers. There are plenty of women programmers and their skills are well recognized. Problems of promotion and status may exist, but that programming is a suitable profession for well-qualified women is not in dispute. The difficulties, and the failure of women to take up the challenge, lie in the field of microcomputers, where the blurred edges between hardware and software, between programming and electronics, tend to turn it into a man's world – and usually a young man's world at that.

## Aspects of microcomputing that match the traditional work pattern of women

### Home based

It seems, then, that many women require work that can be done at least partly from home and that microcomputing offers this facility. This will become increasingly true as more computer systems avail themselves of the telephone networks linking all offices and most homes in the country.

### Skills in communication

Most women have special qualities and a preference for work that requires communicating with other people and for understanding and empathizing with their problems. Microcomputing offers scope for such gifts. The ability to communicate has to extend to encouraging and stimulating others to communicate and must be more than the passing of information in a single direction. At one level, facts and 'specifications' have to be elicited; at another, explanations, solutions and training information has to be imparted; at yet another, communication takes the form of the interchange that leads to sales.

### Systematic approach

The systematic, thorough approach to a problem, which many women have been able to show in other areas of office life is valuable and necessary in microcomputing, not least because it may exercise a beneficial influence on new developments. The concern with how any course of action will affect people themselves has a sobering effect and is needed in the computer world.

### Maturity: an extra advantage

The fact that many women who could today usefully interest themselves in computing are over thirty should be seen as an advantage rather than a disadvantage. The computing industry is unbalanced in age as well as sex, and it is much harder for a man, with his traditional role of breadwinner, to abandon his career and retrain for a new one. A woman, however, often needs to do this when she returns to work after a period of intensive mothering, and often has a good opportunity to do so.

### Time to retrain: a special opportunity for women

Many women are reluctant to return to the same work that they did before giving up full-time employment to have children. Very probably their professional skills will need brushing up, as jobs change over the years. This contributes to the sense of humiliation and worthlessness that many women feel, and which helps the employment market to get away with the downgrading that many women suffer when they return to work. In any case, to return to exactly the same job that was given up some years ago can seem stale and many women are probably suffering at least mildly from the mid-life crisis: loss of confidence and sense of identity as their children grow to be independent of them. Here now is a new skill and one for which they will often have had time to prepare. This is the other side of the coin, for although women often feel trapped in the home, men are in fact far more trapped in a single-career structure and have to be exceptionally bold and adventurous to start something new. Perhaps in twenty or thirty years' time all these re-entering women, having been trained as high-powered computer pro-grammers and operators, will be turning with relief to teaching and social work as a second career subject. It does not matter. The point is that a change is as good as a rest. We have also to remember that society is moving, apparently by design, from the era of the 'caring society' to that of the 'self-help society'. In other words: 'You are on your own. It's up to you'.

Computing, and especially microcomputing, offers a means whereby the wheels of the equal opportunities movement may be turned a little faster, at least as far as women are concerned. Here now, but not to stay, are opportunities for success and excitement such as only ever exist at the start of a new phase of development. It is possible to break into computing with few qualifications and little experience, and without unprecedented abilities or intelligence. Such a situation never lasts for long. Soon the right courses and schools' syllabi will be producing a workforce in large enough numbers to take on the challenge of computing. Unorthodox entries will be less easy; women will not have a scarcity value in the industry; the road to success and interesting jobs will be a stonier one.

*Chapter 2*

# Women are not Taking to Computing: the Evidence

It is everywhere being said that women are not taking to computing. There is some substance in this, although it really depends what is meant by computing, and certainly if word processing is included in the definition, which correctly it is, then women are using computers on a wide and ever-increasing scale. Even so, problems will arise from the failure of women to recognize computers as a general-purpose tool, important in every walk of life, joining reading, writing and arithmetic as traditional basic skills.

Learning to use a computer effectively is different and distinct from learning to program or to follow some activity whose sole concern is computers. The majority of people need to learn only how to use them. If you believe the popular myth that it is unnecessary to know anything about computers in order to be able to use them, then you will wonder what all the fuss is about, since only a tiny fraction of the workforce is needed actually to design, program and service computers. Even learning how to use computers for special applications, rather than learning how to program or design or build them, takes a little application and the more you know, even if only theoretically, about how the machine and operating system work, the less likely you will be to fall into the most obvious traps and the more likely to get good use out of the equipment. Nonetheless, it is also true that using computers in this way involves far less skill and understanding than do the jobs performed by people who work professionally in computing.

*In school*

What is the evidence that women are not taking to computing? It exists and is incontrovertible. Schoolteachers are especially concerned about the failure of girls to take computer studies as an option or even to interest themselves in the computers that have been put into many school libraries in order to make access to them simple. This might not matter if girls were using microcomputers in schools in their free time or in other ways, since much of what is needed on the nursery slopes of computing can be self taught. They are not. Certainly there are a few schools where an imaginative teacher has managed to stimulate the girls into using computers, but in general there is a distressingly low take-up.

At one north London comprehensive school, the current fifth-year computer studies group has no girls at all. The current fourth year shows an improvement with six girls, but alongside them are seventeen boys, so the balance is not equal, although as the balance of boys and girls in the school is unlikely to be equal, it may in fact be better than it looks. The same school had a sixth-form arrangement involving a consortium with two local girls' schools to provide O-level computer studies at this later stage. This had ten girls from girls' schools, two girls from the comprehensive and nine boys. Nineteen passed and although the two failures were female one was a Vietnamese refugee with language difficulties to provide mitigating circumstances. It appears, therefore, that determined efforts on the part of teachers can to some extent counteract the trend, but that the natural tendency is for girls to avoid the subject.

In this same school a computer was available in the library, and here again boys tended to dominate. In the opinion of the deputy head, this was because 'girls were not assertive or confident enough to resist the boys' "helpful" suggestions about programming and gradually the girls would be eased out. Quite curious considering that the same girls were no pushovers in other circumstances, e.g. debating politics.' Girls would not join the lunchtime computer club, but preferred a 'girls only' session after school. It almost seems as if girls object to boys in the context of computing, rather than to computing itself even though these girls are old enough to be interested in boys in other contexts, unlike the nine-to-twelve-year-olds who tend to object to boys as such.

Schools' Inspectors also are getting the impression that girls are failing to seize the opportunity. There seems to be a preponderance of boys even in the more imaginative and exciting courses, using languages like LOGO, designed for primary schools and intended to stimulate children before there is any firmly recognizable division of activities according to gender. Boys in primary schools do needlework, do not yet despise cooking and dancing and, although there is a tendency for girls to be refused places in the school football team, there are still some who want places and enjoy playing. Stereotyping – or perhaps it is voluntary selection of roles – is not yet complete. But still girls are avoiding computers. There are so many aspects of computing that appear to be almost heaven-sent for women that it is hard to believe that it is a natural and inevitable aversion. There must be something prejudicial in the environment.

The figures for girls reading computer studies up to and including A-level show that, although girls are not turning in great numbers to this kind of computing (which is not the same as learning to use one for practical purposes), the figures are no worse than for physics or technical drawing, slightly worse than for maths and considerably worse than for chemistry.*

## Out of school

Children and parents can improve their computing skills while enjoying themselves at holiday camps in the traditional American style, although, once again, fewer girls than boys are taking up these opportunities. Here I suspect we have two problems. One is that boys take more naturally to computers than girls. The other is that at a certain age girls find boys positively antipathetic and shy away from boy-dominated activities. It is then too late to enter the field on an equal footing and so they appear to be permanently disadvantaged. Thus the situation is self-perpetuating. Because most girls tend not to know as much about computers as boys, those who do have a battle to establish the fact, and tend either to become aggressive and show off about it, or to take the traditional female course of opting out.

## After school: re-training youth

Opportunities for re-training or for further training after leaving school are not being taken up by many girls. As these short training course are often in skills like word processing, which have traditionally been the domain of women, there must be a risk that women will start to lose dominance even in such areas. Maybe in a world of equal opportunities, and if women had no special talent for those skills that are required to run an office well, this would be a desirable trend and one that would move women from being concentrated in low-status jobs into a more equal spread across all jobs – although I doubt it myself, as I think that probably more women than men have a special aptitude for office work. The obsessional qualities necessary to a really good secretary/administrator, the attention to detail and constant questioning as to how a given change or action or decision will affect people or the running of the system – all these are found more frequently in women than in men.

An article in *Computing* entitled 'A second chance for GLC School Leavers'† describes the efforts of the Information Technology Centres to provide computing skills for youngsters who have not acquired them at school. The manager of Brixton Itec 'is rather concerned about the lack of female

*WISE 84, an Equal Opportunities Commission/Engineering Council project, publishes the figures for girls' and boys' school examination results in 1980

†December 1983

applicants. In his next intake he has one girl – they are just not interested enough to apply.' The manager of Southwark Itec goes further, saying, 'If you recognize that girls are just not applying then you've got to do something. It would be the same if young black kids weren't applying here. We would have to go out and find them and make sure they apply. So I think we must make a national effort to attract women.' He even recommends positive discrimination. In the same article, children who were interviewed revealed that they had had opportunities to learn about computers at school but had found the teaching methods boring or unstimulating. 'It was the lessons and the way the teachers taught them. I had no drive to learn.' 'Well, I can usually pick things up quickly but I had problems at school. I got bored quickly and then I got uptight and then I got into trouble with the teachers.'

TOPS courses are linked to the sixty-nine Government Skill Centres. In 1980-1 only 4 per cent of places at these were filled by women. Womens' groups are attempting to communicate with and inspire women all over the country to consider 'non-traditional' careers and re-training. Further details are given in Chapter 13.

## University education

At university level, because computing is more often provided with science than with arts courses, some girls are drawn in, but it is a well-established fact that fewer girls than men read science subjects and so the failure of the schools is compounded.

At degree level the same disparity appears, though in fact it is possible to enter programming from a number of other disciplines, not all of which are scientific.

## At work

The number of women in the workforce using computers is more difficult to guess. Women are accepted and established in the field of computer programming, and although their numbers may not equal those of men, there is no doubt about their equality of skill. The present chairman of the Computer Services Association, one of the most powerful bodies in the business, is a woman and at meetings, though there are often few women in the audience, they are usually well represented on the platform. F International (see Chapter 5) is a body that employs approximately 800 'highly skilled information-processing technicians'. The company also offers employees 'an opportunity to continue working within the computer industry on a part-time basis and from their own home base... in the main this means married women with young children'. There are others working in the organization – 'disabled applicants, men and women looking after elderly parents and people following "unusual" careers'.

The number of women using computers at work is obscured by the fact that the people who take purchasing decisions and the managers are most often men. Customers in computer salesrooms are often men purchasing equipment for their secretaries to use; only occasionally are they women – usually professional women, researchers, doctors and so forth – and on rare occasions secretaries who have been sent by enlightened bosses to try out the computers and discuss their practical anxieties with sales' staff before a purchase is made. On the surface, then, it can appear that computer-users in the workforce are almost entirely men. This is, of course, quite a false picture, because as yet far more secretaries and typists are using computers for word processing than managers are using them for administrative and financial management, although this is an area of use that will grow.

Women have, in fact, responded well to the use of computers in office work. This is true of all ages: it is not confined to young women who might be considered less set in their ways than their older colleagues. It is generally recognized that new things are harder for older people to learn, but the achievement of the older age group in learning to use computers is good. It has, however, been largely unwitting. For some reason the general public and office staff have been deluded into thinking that a dedicated word processor is not a computer, though indisputably it is. Whether there would have been more difficulty in getting people to use word processors had they been called computers we shall never know. A few years ago the term 'word processor' was as incomprehensible and alarming to most people as 'computer' is now, although it does convey the notion of being helpful in a particular context. Be that as it may, a problem now exists, as regular users of word processors react with horror to the notion of computing on the grounds that it is much too technical and difficult for them to understand. Although using a word-processing package on a general-purpose computer is slightly more complicated than using a word-processor package on a computer dedicated to that task, the person capable of using the latter has by definition sufficient intelligence and initiative to use the former. It is using one at all that takes a little concentration, in the early stages at least, but very soon becomes second nature on either type of machine.

## Women in the computer industry itself

At computer exhibitions and showrooms there is always a preponderance of men, but increasingly women are also present. Women are also beginning to operate most professionally as sales representatives. For this it is essential to know what a machine can do and to pull together a certain amount of technical understanding, but it is not necessary to be able to operate it yourself. A traditional sales approach involves conversation and description with no more than the most limited kind of demonstration. Often women are as good as, or better than, men at this and I shall develop this theme in a later chapter. It is still fairly rare to find women who are technically competent.

The question of whether women are succeeding in using computers should not be confused with the question of whether women are succeeding in general. It is irrelevant to connect the fact that women are not to be found in large numbers in positions of senior management or jobs with high status because the men in these positions, though some are struggling gallantly with the appalling task which faces them, are in general doing pretty badly at computing as well. Many large firms are seriously embarrassed by the task of re-educating senior management, so at this level the problems are not confined to women. In the younger age groups, however, they are, and this is more serious, as it means that unless some remedy is found the weakness will not be bred out of the system by the passage of time.

### The reasons

If we have proved beyond reasonable doubt that computing is an ideal occupation for women and that women are not taking to it in any numbers, then the next question must be: why? There is no single answer to this and to find even a composite answer we must look in various directions.

*Innate capacity*
Before discussing valid causes any suggestion that the reasoning, logical or mathematical abilities of women as a group are in some way unsuited to computing or inferior to those of men must be dismissed. There may be cultural or genetic reasons that make women turn away from such subjects,[2] but brainpower is not in dispute. It is true that there is an argument about the right and left sides of the brain and the fact that one is more responsible for abilities related to the perception of spatial concepts and the analysis of data (e.g. maths and chess), whereas the other is more responsible for abilities connected with verbalization and communication of data.[3] Computing is a discipline that requires some (but not necessarily great) mathematical ability, logic, which seems to span the two areas, and a grasp of the principles of language systems and communication methods. Thus it undoubtedly could not be said to fall wholly into either of the two 'sides-of-the-brain' groups of abilities. This is particularly so in view of recent discussion of the sides of the brain, which is even now throwing up the idea that women may even have a better biological integration of the two types of intelligence than men have.[4,5]

One of the first people, in fact, to grasp the concepts of computing was Ada Augusta, Countess of Lovelace, daughter of Lord Byron. She became a close friend and confidant of Charles Babbage,* inventor of the first analytical computer. Babbage is said to have failed to explain his invention even to his colleagues and was unable to speak with coherence in public. Dr B.V. Bowden in his history of computation,[6] quotes a contemporary description of Ada's first meeting with the 'Analytical Engine', as Babbage's computer was called, and adds his own wry comment: 'While the rest of the party gazed at this beautiful instrument with the same sort of expression and feeling that

* 1792–1871

some savages are said to have shown on first seeing a looking-glass or hearing a gun, Miss Byron, young as she was, understood its working and saw the great beauty of the invention.' Ada's aptitude for 'grasping the strong points and real difficulties of first principles' was remarked upon, and her association with Babbage was quite close. She translated a paper by Menabrea entitled 'A Sketch of the Analytical Engine invented by Charles Babbage' and it is said that her translation, to which great value was added by her comprehensive notes and a series of examples of its use, shows her to have had 'a remarkable understanding of Babbage's ideas, which she explained far more clearly than Babbage himself ever seems to have done.' Ada collaborated with Babbage on various schemes and is said to have persuaded him to abandon the decimal system in favour of the binary, which now underpins all modern thinking about computers.

Nor was Ada simply a freak. Her friends and advisers included Mrs Somerville, after whom the Oxford college was named, Mrs de Morgan, wife of the famous mathematician Augustus de Morgan, and her own mother, Annabella Milbanke, who was a mathematician, and to whom Byron (who soon regretted his marriage, referred as the 'Princess of Parallelograms'.* Another member of this gifted circle was Mary Shelley, daughter of Mary Wollstonecraft and William Godwin and wife of the poet. As well as displaying her understanding of many of the concepts of chemistry and mathematics in her book *Frankenstein*, she portrayed, well ahead of modern science-fiction writers, a Fifth Generation creature, a bemused and artificially intelligent being, created by man and feared by his creator. She wrote of science with a feeling for the subject that equals that of most men: 'In other studies you go as far as others have gone before you and there is nothing more to know; but in a scientific pursuit there is continual food for discovery and wonder.'

*The practical approach and a concern with people*
If we accept that the root cause of women's failure to take to computing is not natural inferiority, then we must look for other reasons. First, there are characteristics in women themselves which, linked with the way computers are generally presented and thought of, make for a predisposition to reject the whole subject.

John Stuart Mill says that, for whatever reason, 'looking at women as they are known in experience, it may be said of them, that the general bent of their talent is toward the practical.'* Later he refers to 'this sensibility to the present' and adds that, whereas men can get carried away by speculative ideas, women 'discern and discriminate the particular cases in which general principles are and are not applicable.... A woman seldom runs wild after an abstraction. The habitual direction of her mind to dealing with things as individuals rather than in groups and her more lively interest in the present feelings of persons, which makes her consider first of all, in anything which

*The Subjection of Women

claims to be applied to practice, in what manner persons will be affected by it – these two things make her extremely unlikely to put faith in any speculation which loses sight of individuals, and deals with things as if they existed for the benefit of some imaginary entity, some mere creation of the mind, not resolvable into the feelings of living beings'.

This, I am sure, is how many women view computers. Whereas men will embrace the idea of computers, running wild after an abstraction, and later find that they can also be put to numerous uses, women will not exert themselves until they see some point. A machine over which their sons and husbands pore, apparently involved only in playing shoot-and-kill games or programming it to ask your name seems utterly pointless. Even high resolution graphics, drawing flowers and birds flying round the screen, tends to provoke the response, 'Yes, it's brilliant, but what can you do with it?' The in-group jargon and competitiveness about amounts of memory, degrees of resolution, speed and the amount of noise that can be generated by any particular machine does not appeal to women. Female competitiveness usually takes a more subtle form.

In a study carried out in the London Borough of Croydon on behalf of the Equal Opportunities Commission, fifteen-year-old girls were asked to comment on the computer studies courses. Asked if the course had turned out as they expected they replied that, on the whole, it had not. They had expected to be taught more practical uses for computers, more about actual programming; they found it to be much more complicated, detailed and theoretical than they had imagined, with not enough practice. This can be summed up as a plea to stop talking about computers and begin doing something.

Suggested changes to the courses were: more practical programming, more active lessons to create greater interest on the pupil's part, and more explanation of computer language and terms.

*Presentation of the subject in educational and other literature*
If women are to be attracted to the idea of computing they must first be shown some good reason. This point overlaps with the argument about general presentation and advertising of computers, but is a special case when we are considering education, as education is usually a public service with obligations other than simple market forces. The way in which computers are presented in advertising and in education catches the attention of men and is very antipathetic to most women and girls. The study for the Equal Opportunities Commission quoted above looked at both literature and teaching materials to see how the subject was presented. A review of the kind of books that might be used as teaching aids (and in a new field teachers do not have a lot of choice) showed that nearly all had a heavy preponderance of men or boys in the illustrations and that where a woman was shown it was usually as a low-status 'operator', sometimes with a man shown giving her

directions. Some contained openly sexist statements and even the BBC Radiovision series produced in 1982 clearly identified some tasks as 'women's work'. These things taken in isolation may seem unimportant, but taken right across the board they help to reinforce stereotypes that are already established in other ways and deter girls from reaching out for male-dominated professions. Computer graphics, with tedious frequency, are used to draw feminine shapes. There must surely be other shapes worth reproducing on all this high-powered equipment? However little men understand the reasons, it is a fact that these things offend some girls and women, and that is sufficient reason for choosing alternatives.

It is a well-established and documented fact that the performance or achievement of an individual, and especially a child, is strongly affected by the expectation that 'relevant others' show. The power of suggestion is much stronger than the power of self-confidence and self-image, and self-confidence is itself partly a creation of the mirror image, the reflection of the value in which others hold us. It is an unusual degree of self-confidence or motivation that distinguishes artists from normal citizens and allows them to persevere in the face of lack of recognition in the present. Most women are bound to be affected by the view that men take of their general abilities in this kind of field, and there are many examples of women in senior positions who have been taken for secretaries, addressed as 'Dear' and asked to do some photocopying by male colleagues unaware of their status. How much more, then, are girls in school, still searching for an identity and sense of self, likely to be affected by teachers' expectations, conscious or unconscious?

## The socialization of boys and men

*In school*

This topic merges with the second group of reasons for women being put off the idea of computing and is located not so much in characteristics that pertain to women themselves, but rather those that pertain to men and boys. Here again the report on the Croydon schools shows that girls find that the behaviour of boys, which is often the way they are expected/encouraged to behave, is a deterrent to involvement with the computer. Professor Tessa Blackstone, in her essay on 'The Education of Girls Today'[8] comments that the unequal treatment of boys and girls has the result that 'control over one's destiny and one's access to power and prestige will vary according to whether one is male or female.... A further result, so far as women are concerned... is that it encourages women in general to undervalue themselves.' In the Croydon study a number of the researchers observed that a common pattern in the classrooms is for boys to enter first and sit near the front in a group. Their names are called first on the register and they are given the worksheets first. One researcher commented that girls were noticeable by their lack of involvement and another that in one class a boy asked the same question every week: 'Sir, why can't we have more boys in this group?'

Here it seems that the teachers (usually, but not always, male) are as much to blame as the boys; from which it can be concluded that the general characteristics observable in the behaviour of males are as likely to be the result of socialization, not genetics, as those observed in the behaviour of females.

Computer clubs are on offer in many schools. Again, these are generally dominated by boys even where girls attend to start off with. It is only fair to say, however, that in some schools teachers (often male) have made strenuous efforts to provide facilities for girls at separate times, or on a strictly supervized time-sharing basis.

It is interesting to put all this discussion of the use of computers in co-educational schools into context by comparison with a single-sex girls' school. At St Paul's Girls' School in London computer studies is not taken as a public examination subject. This may reflect the distressing fact that it is not, as laid down in the syllabus, a subject thought suitable for the brighter children in any school and St Paul's takes its entry from a highly selected group of girls. It is, however, taught as a compulsory subject in the first year and is soon to be included in the second. The school has six BBC micros and small classes. These younger girls are described as 'very keen' on computers, usually getting to lessons early in order to get started. Some of them have found the concepts of programming quite hard to grasp, and their teacher finds, contrary to the common view, that this is often related to mathematical ability. She feels that girls and women do not in general have the same wild enthusiasm for the computer as men do – a difference that she perceives even between herself and the men teachers at the school.

In the sixth form, computing has also been introduced as part of a general studies course. Here the problem is that the girls have a heavy workload from their other subjects and are not prepared to put in all the extra time that is really necessary to 'take off' with the computer. Their teacher believes that boys would probably apportion their time differently.

There are also four computer club sessions held each week in the lunch hour and attendance is voluntary. They are always full – twelve children in each, two to each computer. This is a school, therefore, where no special measures have been taken to encourage girls, as none were needed. The Croydon report mentions one school where much attention had been paid to this, as at the north London school discussed earlier.

*In society and at work*
Studies seem to show, then, that schoolgirls of various ages withdraw from what they regard as the oppressively know-all behaviour of boys where computers are concerned; so what about adults? Here similar assumptions of women's technical incompetence, or of computing being a 'man's world' also seem to be made – not aggressively, but unthinkingly – and women passively allow it to happen, though they sometimes jib at a later stage. A very high

proportion of the men who buy computers are buying them for their women employees to use. It is unusual for a boss who wishes his secretaries to use a micro as a word processor to send them to view the equipment and make choices themselves. Since the men often know practically nothing when they first come in, this cannot be because the women lack expertise to any greater degree than they do.

There are numerous instances of the wrong equipment having been chosen for an office and others where, although the secretary could be won over to the idea of a computer if the situation were properly handled, the damage is done at an early stage by the tactless and inconsiderate behaviour of her boss, who then loses out by her refusal to co-operate.

In society generally, men are assumed not to be the ones who know about computers, since few people do, but to be the ones who make decisions. This assumption operates strongly in most homes, is not successfully counteracted at school and is certainly prevalent in the business world. In firms large enough to have a member of staff assigned to look after micros it is not necessarily always a man who is chosen, but this is most likely to be because such a position goes to someone with a computer science degree, and a degree more or less cancels out the sex differential.

*Advertising*
Computer advertising is aimed almost exclusively at men, with women only involved as sex objects (as with car advertising) or as rather unattractive pseudo-men. Danielle Bernstein complains about this in *Practical Computing*.*She has analysed advertisements and found three types: 'men as decision makers; women as attention getters and family oriented ads which do not include the whole family'. Where women are included in advertisements they are shown only in charge of very young children. After the age of ten, women disappear and girls, if shown, are watching the boys admiringly. Ms Bernstein finds, however, that advertisements are beginning to change and to include women more often. The increased use of television for advertising computers recently has shown examples of this. One advertisement showed two parents, with mother playing a full part in the operations, creeping down to use the home computer when they thought that the children were not around. This may be partly as a result of Ms Bernstein's own efforts, for as she warns the manufacturers and advertisers: 'the potential market is 50 per cent female. Don't alienate us.'

The sole purpose of advertisements is to make money and the reason for beginning to include women in the target is either that advertisers are discovering that women do affect sales in some way, or that they need new markets and are trying to stimulate women into purchasing computers. Certainly women are an important influence in the home-computer market, though perhaps only recently so. The maternal instinct is very powerful and in

*January 1984

modern times it takes a resourceful woman to equip her family properly for the life ahead of them. Once she has recognized that a knowledge of computing is necessary for her children's success and survival at work, then she will take the appropriate steps. The appropriate steps do not at the moment seem to include learning about computers for herself – or even effecting the purchase – because she is usually convinced that such a course is beyond her ability. However, there is evidence that this, too, will change soon, as an ever-increasing number of wives have now taken the decision to go on courses and tackle the subject, judging that the time has come to take the bull by the horns.

*Presentation of uses and purpose of learning about computers*
Women have not yet been shown practical reasons for exerting themselves where computers are concerned. This may be the fault of advertising and presentation, but it is partly also the fault of women themselves, as the general failure of women to involve themselves in science and scientific subjects makes it harder for them to see the uses of computers, which are easily obscured by the complexity and novelty of the subject. There is a confusion between the use of computers as tools to provide things that are to do with computers, such as programs or better computers; the use of computer studies in school as a mind-training discipline; and the use of computers as tools to provide an almost indefinite list of services unconnected with computing as such – for example, word processing, accounts and financial management, analysis of research data, printing of labels for commercial goods, a substitute for telex and telegrams, control of automated processes in factories and assembly lines, a tool for graphic design, kitchen planning, aids to diagnosis in medicine or to planning timetables in schools, and many, many more. The third group of uses – services – is the one that affects 90 per cent of the population, men and women, and is the one least likely to be provided by the home-computer – 'toys-for-boys' – market. However, home computers are a way of getting started and should certainly not be despised.

To sum up, it seems that the reasons for women not being as readily attracted to computers as men are connected with social attitudes and that these reinforce in women a diffidence and reluctance to become involved. Exacerbating factors can be observed in our educational system, in our family lives, in the commercial approach to the subject and in the reaction and in the assumptions of women's role and abilities frequently made by both men and women. It is possible that there is a genetic base to the factors that make men and women differ in their interests and their achievements in scientific and related fields, but it seems more likely that it is a self-perpetuating situation that is very largely the result of social conditioning. In either case, it is important that the prevailing trend should be reduced either to nothing or at least to its natural proportions, if such there be. Schools, society, advertising and commercial agencies all need to alter their habits, as do women themselves, as much for their own practical advantage as for any idealogical principles.

*Chapter 3*

# Suggested Remedies

Remedial measures must necessarily be as complex and wide reaching as the problems themselves. In fact, for older women it may well be difficult to find sure remedies, but this makes it all the more urgent that we provide prophylactics for the workers of the future. The most important area for change is therefore education. This is not because it is necessarily the most to blame for the current situation; social attitudes – and that means families, which in turn means women themselves – are even more pervasive than schools in the conditioning that they bring about. In the Croydon schools cited in the previous chapter it was found that the middle-class boys were more prepared than their working-class schoolmates to envisage girls using the computer – an indication that awareness of the problems is greater in middle-class households, where sex stereotyping is generally much less prevalent.

## Education

It is far beyond the scope of this book to suggest specific remedies for changing social attitudes. It is possible, however, to make suggestions about what could be done in schools, and also in commerce and advertising, as social attitudes are inevitably influenced by advertising and the way that the media presents a subject.

Under conditions of general unemployment such as we are experiencing at the moment, many people think seriously that women should be discouraged from working to leave more jobs for men, the traditional breadwinners. Quite apart from whether women have a right to work or not, however, they do have a vital contribution to make to today's society. If some people only are working, then they must earn enough to keep the rest. In order to develop industry and fight the battle for national survival we need the best people in those critical jobs that require the highest talent. Fifty per cent of these will be women. John Nicholson, in his excellent and readable book *Men and Women*, stresses that the most talented women are more talented than the average man and thus, even if on average women appear (for reasons that are almost certainly socially induced) to be less able at scientific subjects, we cannot afford the loss of vital talent that is a consequence of discouraging women in the way that we do.

Professor Cooper, head of Organization Psychology at Manchester University, is quoted as saying 'As for industry, why not encourage the women? The male manager is terrible – he's been screwing up industry for the last 20 years.'* He goes further and declares that:

> Men are more ambitious than women. They just don't happen to be as good as the women. To them a job has to be done because it might advance their career. A woman says 'I want to do this job to my satisfaction.' She is generally more concerned about the people around her, being particularly concerned with the well being of her subordinates. Interestingly our research shows that male subordinates perceive their female bosses as more successful than men and better than men in the management of people.

Professor Tessa Blackstone comments that 'the economic benefits of further education for women are almost certainly underestimated by employers.' She, like Professor Cooper, is referring to a wider field than simply computing or technology, but there are echoes of John Stuart Mill's judgements in these statements, which bear out the argument, not that women are better, but that they have something different, complementary and valuable to offer.

Let us look, then, at the suggestions and recommendations that have been made in the literature for improving the situation in schools. Professor Blackstone recommends far more careful guidance and encouragement of girls, particularly in secondary education, as this seems to be where the rot sets in. The Equal Opportunities Commission provides a set of guidelines for Local Education Authorities, for schools and for teachers. The guidelines for the LEAs include developing plans to attract and train the right kind of teachers and to include IT training in compulsory teachers' training courses. Schools are advised to think out their use of computers in the curriculum and it is suggested that the provision of 'the necessary knowledge, skills and experience' might be best in a separately timetabled subject in order to avoid

*The Guardian

concentrating them in subjects that are regarded as boys' domain.

> The school should ensure that girls are not discriminated against by: an option scheme which makes the choice of Computer Studies difficult for girls; unstructured or unsupervized club activities where aggresive boys take a disproportionate share of available resources; undue linking of Information Technology with what are seen as boys' activities by the choice of staff, location or subject matter.

The guidelines for the teacher include advice about the careful selecting of teaching materials that avoid too close a link with mathematics and avoid traditional stereotypes; leading discussions in such a way that girls are involved as much as boys; laying out the classroom and organizing the teaching programme in a way that helps other staff and parents to be aware of IT, does not place girls at the back of the class and allows them to give each other moral support, does not use posters or examples of work that do not give a fair representation of the contribution of both sexes, and includes girls in extra-curricular activities.

These are all useful suggestions. They are aimed, however, at reducing male dominance more perhaps than at increasing the level of female interest. I am sure that there are also ways of making computers and technology more positively appealing to girls and women. Computing can be amazingly interesting, fascinating and exciting once one gets involved in the subject and if one is able to get a glimpse of the fun it can be. The title of Peter Laurie's book, *The Joy of Computing,** is intended to convey some of this. The presentation of computers at the moment is, from a female point of view, dreary, with too much emphasis on killing games, maths and memory. It is not games as such that alienate girls: there just needs to be some better ones. The computerization of *The Hobbit* is a start, and there are plenty of other games and stories that could be treated similarly, including games of skill involving more neutral subjects than bomb and kill. Even games of mystery and detection would be more appealing.

As well as games, there is also the introduction to the real meaning of computers and computer power. If programming could be taught in an interesting way, there is no reason why girls would not enjoy it as much as boys and benefit from it equally. If we consider the skills that go into programming, and what has to be developed as one learns to program, then it would be a wonderfully modern, practical and clearly worthwhile subject with which to fill the gap left in the curriculum by the departure of Latin as a general mind-training compulsory subject. Moreover, if done carefully, it could continue to be linked with maths. Many mathematical concepts that seem obscure or meaningless at school reveal their full usefulness in the context of computing when it becomes necessary to understand them in order to write a program or master some aspect of using a computer. Such

*Hutchinson, 1983

concepts as *xy* co-ordinates, matrices and vectors, number systems, boolean algebra, mathematical logic, modulus and simple calculation itself all play an essential part in computing. Learning their practical application not only brings about a clearer appreciation of the principles of mathematics, but also makes the whole subject much less arid and frightening than it often is in its traditional classroom presentation.

Finally, I think that computing should soon be treated as the fourth R, as something which is a general-purpose skill, taught in the early years as a separate subject and later used in every subject. If computing is incorporated right across the curriculum in this way, then there are opportunities at all levels for girls. In any case, it ought immediately to be made an integral part of the commerce departments and the subjects which are traditionally girls' subjects, like typing (word processing) and book keeping (computerized accounts) and so forth. The reason that this is not done is primarily that computers are expensive, but it seems criminal to teach girls outdated methods that will be of little use to them in the outside world.

An article in *The Guardian**\* echoes and expands this point, talking this time about higher education. It describes a scheme funded by IBM to extend the teaching of the use of computers to practical subjects like engineering. 'For the majority of young people this should be what they are looking for in their post-school studies – the computer or computer-based equipment and training on it is just as essential as the library and/or the laboratory, whether they are studying archaeology, accountancy, business studies, economics, music, zoology or whatever. For the key point is that computers are only tools.'

I am suggesting, therefore, that, as well as taking practical measures to try to counteract the almost instinctive favouring of boys in the way in which computers are treated at school (and at home), computers should be used as part of a three-pronged attack on education in order to improve education as well as to spread the knowledge of computing. The first part of the attack is to teach programming and computer science in an interesting, relevant and stimulating way. Most students enjoy a mental challenge if it is interestingly presented. The second is to use computing as a general-purpose tool, similar to reading and writing. The third is to build on those areas where computers are already being usefully applied in the outside world, many of which are already areas in which women traditionally dominate, such as the subjects that come under the heading of Commerce and Office Training. More and more, computers will be useful to nurses, social workers, medical secretaries and teachers, as well as to clerical and office workers as at present. If schools are to equip girls properly for the future, even in a traditional way, they will inevitably need to teach them to use computers.

\*14 February 1984

## Sales and advertising; social attitudes

Sales and advertising campaigns currently are aimed almost exclusively at men. The people who prepare the copy and pursue the sales are not influenced by social oughts but by the need to make sales and money with which to continue in business. Once women start to take an interest in computers and demonstrate that they are a market force, then the advertisements and sales campaigns will be aimed at women as well as men. There are no specific recommendations that one can make, because the market will find its own way soon enough. Protests by women and articles such as the one that I have quoted from by Danielle Bernstein (p.31) may draw copy writers' and manufacturers' attention to the fact that women are a market force if it is true that they are; otherwise, they will have no effect. Similarly, although social attitudes to a certain extent dictate behaviour, they also arise from it. If women continue their efforts to affect the conditioning and upbringing of both girls and boys in their care, then social attitudes will continue to change even more than they have done already, and the problem will gradually evaporate.

## Working for changes in women themselves

Whereas a few women seem to take a stance that is so aggressive that it seems to some people to be counter-productive, it is also the case that very many women make it difficult for men to behave other than as they do. The 'little woman' act is a very powerful one, and the role is instinctive to many women. Some people think that it is a natural part of the special characteristics of women that I have mentioned, the 'special comforting, civilizing function' which Katharine Whitehorn mentions in her *Observer* articles. Personally, I do not see why it is necessary to resort to rushing round making cups of coffee for healthy men of no special status in the firm, or resorting to direct sexual flirtation and manipulation, in order to prove that you are worth employing or to gain some particular end when there are many other methods that are just as easy and less needlessly self-abasing or distracting. This is particularly so because once you adopt the pose of being helpless except at typing or coffee-making or whatever, then the attitude spills over to thinking or pretending that you are hopeless at everything practical; or that if you are not especially talented in that direction it is not something which you could, with an effort, overcome just like any other obstacle. Many men sidestep the things of which they are nervous (including learning about new technology), but they either do it quietly and without drawing attention to themselves, or decide to make a positive virtue of their ignorance and trumpet aloud their claim to be arts graduates with no knowledge of science. Women often encourage men to think that they are helpless,[9] or not as good at driving cars, mending machines or using computers and acquire discredit rather than praise. Men who are bad at these things, and there are many, either deny it or turn it into an asset.

What steps might be open to women who are interested in establishing skills in some area of computing? Perhaps some of the groups of women who set up co-operative child-minding schemes, with, for example, one morning on and four off in return for looking after five toddlers, could jointly purchase a computer and share the use and the learning. The early stages, and programming in general, are best done in company. Such a purchase could be justified in lots of ways: self-improvement for those who wish to pursue further education courses; preparation for educating children later; after a while, earning small additions to the family income; helping with voluntary and political organizations in the chore of record-keeping and envelope-addressing; and so on. Finance could be shared; any sum divided among a group is more manageable than it is for a single budget.

The South Glamorgan Women's Workshop is one instance of a group that has started a beginners' computing course for women. There are three electronics tutors among the staff and nursery facilities are provided free. An article in *The Guardian** describes the course as being 'practical in orientation' with a period of work experience in the computer industry. 'It is intended to build women's confidence by easing them gently into a work situation after years of unemployment or motherhood, while also offering the experience necessary to impress subsequent employers.' This excellent enterprise is funded by the European Social Fund and South Glamorgan County Council.

Haringey Women's Training and Education Centre offers a number of stimulating activities and courses to women. One of the examples of women who have helped themselves given later in this book (see Chapter 7-9), used the Haringey facilities. Such facilities vary a little from one borough or education authority to another, but by and large the country is beginning to be fairly well served. Public libraries and notice boards are a source of information about what is available.

Most local authorities, polytechnics or evening institutes now provide some kind of introductory computer courses and some of these are intended for parents and their children to attend together. This is a good way for a self-conscious woman to start; she can always pretend that she is just doing it to help her child. Women are too often conditioned to think of themselves as providers and enablers rather than as individuals with rights as well as obligations. This is not necessarily undesirable and may be what makes girls usually gentler and less obstreperous than boys, but it makes it difficult for women to reach out and grasp for themselves. This is why it can be a good idea to learn partly for family benefit and partly for yourself.

There is a network of self-help groups organized through *Personal Computer World* and entitled 'Computertown UK'. Details of groups in any

*10 January 1984

particular neighbourhood can be obtained through *PCW*, which is one of the most popular microcomputing monthly magazines. Many areas have micro clubs and many organizations, such as the Genealogical Association or the Society of Indexers, have groups and meetings to promote exchange of ideas and information among members. Scratch your professional or voluntary organization and you will very likely find a micro-users' club. The language is a little hard to learn at first but the natives are very friendly and longing to share their expertise and their pleasures with newcomers.

*Chapter 4*

# Future Patterns

*Social and occupational patterns*
It is interesting to realize that the pattern of work that could develop as a result
of the impact of new technology is not, if we take a longer view, a new one at
all. Before the Industrial Revolution, the earliest origins of which are rarely
placed before the mid-eighteenth century, the traditional place of work was
the home. Sometimes the work was organized in family units and sometimes
in larger units – groups of families – in what would nowadays be considered a
small geographical area, working for an employer who provided them with
work, raw materials and sometimes equipment as well. Pauline Gregg, in her
*Social and Economic History of England,**  writes: 'Until the middle of the
eighteenth century woollen manufacture was England's chief industry....
Originally the weaving of cloth had been carried on in the homes of the
people for household needs. But the stage was soon reached when the cloth
was taken to market and sold for use in other parts of the country or for
export.' She adds that small masters organized the work through their families
and neighbours. Women and children played an active part in the work from
a very early age. It is known that the architecture of the cottages in the wool
districts was affected by the industry carried on within them. The woollen
trade was already considerably capitalized and organized before the Industrial

*Harrap, 1982

Revolution, but still most work was done at home. The other important industry, agriculture, was also based on or near the home and included women in various roles.

The Industrial Revolution caused the traditional cottage- and craft-based industries to be superseded by production methods that required intensive capital. The cost and often the size of the equipment made it essential that workers be gathered together to work in one place – the site of the equipment rather than their homes. Even before this period, women had tended to carry out different types of work from men and sexual division of labour was not a new phenomenon. But now the family and the work that women could easily do in conjunction with 'their very special responsibility for society's well-being'[10] was split from the work that men could do. They were employed in factories and for a terrible period women and children also worked in mines; at that time working conditions for everyone were horrific by any standards. However, it gradually came to be accepted that, because work was now usually an away-from-home activity and women with small children had a special role in the home, then women were less likely to have careers. Work they may, and always have done to a certain extent, but their work has usually been deemed less skilled and less important than that of men, and to this day they tend to be paid less.

It is possible, even probable, that even if women move into computing on a large scale and that this makes it possible for them to carry out skilled work from home, nonetheless men will continue to dominate and earn more. It all depends whether the characteristics that are currently observable in women are inherent or are culturally acquired. *The Times** reports a recent survey of software workers in the USA which shows that 'job satisfaction has very little to do with pay levels' and that when 'all the factors of education and position within the hierarchies of software workers are taken into account women will get only 59% of the pay men get.' The survey also points out that 'to put a dollar value on pay discrimination, on average it is a $5000 liability to be a woman in software'.† This study shows that 24 per cent of the software workforce in the United States is female, 'that software is the hightec field most open to women, yet their status is that of second-class citizens. . . . For whatever reason, software has replicated the sexual (and racial) divisions that characterize older professions'. This is discouraging, but at least there are women in software, which is more than can be said for women in large numbers in many other professions. If women go into traditional computing as an organized profession the results will probably be as predicted. Computing can be used in an unconventional way to gain status in other professions, to set up your business and charge your own fees and also to continue to find employment in a world where the increase in unemployment is likely to hit women harder than men.

*13 December 1983

†*Computing*, 9 February 1984; survey by Kraft and Dubnoff

That the average earnings of women are lower than those of men is not necessarily, as may at first appear, the result of a male chauvinist plot, but is because women tend to be specialists and programmers while men are managers. It may be that women are being blocked from management, but this is unlikely. Some women prefer to do a job that has satisfaction and clear merits rather than organizing groups of people to do interesting work which they themselves are frustrated from doing by their managerial positions. Other women, who could perhaps make good managers, are inhibited from seeking such promotion because of the burdens of their dual role and their wish to put their families high in their set of priorities. The above article ends, quoting the survey: ' "With respect to gender, if generalists are rewarded with higher pay than specialists, then the generalists tend to be men while the specialists tend to be women. In programming we have not found any evidence of a strong relationship between technical skill and high pay." Despite these discrepancies, job satisfaction is high.'

Later in the chapter we look in detail at one organization that employs women on their own terms and raises the hypothesis at least that women may have something special to contribute at management level. Here again it could be argued that the unused resource of women workers is qualitative as well as quantitative.

If a return to more opportunities for work based at home, or to work that can be done partly at home and partly at a place of work outside the home is postulated, then women have an opportunity to be in the vanguard, to show the way. If they do not lead, they will have to follow later, as it seems certain that there will be changes and that, although men's work patterns are set in more traditional moulds and they are in general less flexible and adaptable, nevertheless they will get there in the end and women will have missed another opportunity to take the lead, to gain some status.

Janet Radcliffe Richards, in her excellent book *The Sceptical Feminist,** observes that in any industrialized society whatever women choose to do tends to become low status. This is supported by evidence from anthropological studies. Computing and its related skills (except the Cinderellas like word processing, which, though highly skilled in its more advanced forms, stems from typing and therefore already carries the stigma of female occupation), are so highly regarded – or ludicrously overrated – and so apparently fascinating to men that there is more chance that they will not be downgraded by being associated with women.

The kind of hardware and software that is being developed at the moment, with facilities for linking up micros and small pieces of equipment suitable to the cottage industry, to large and expensive machinery suitable to an office or laboratory, using something as readily available and simple to operate as the telephone system – national and international – helps to conjure up a vision

*Penguin, 1982

of a new organization of work and society. The vision still has large firms and capital investment, but it has satellite rings of workers operating remote from the central organization. There are still managers and hierarchies: we are not all our own masters. However, there will be more variety and more shades of partnership. There may be more self-employed but some home workers, though they may own their own equipment, will sell their services to a middle-man and charge a special rate; others will sell only their labour as they do today, but they may have some choice and variety about when and where they work because firms will see the benefits of providing equipment or loaning out portable sets; travelling people, such as salesmen, will work by going out from home and communicating the fruits of their travels to a central computer staffed by workers who turn up according to schedule as they do now; some jobs will still require a gathering of the workforce in a central location.

Jane Wilkinson, Group Personnel and Training Manager for F International, (see p.45) writing in *Data Processing*,* points out that:

> Many of the current social and technological trends may produce an equally dramatic re-direction in the pattern of work.
> Information technology has removed many of the reasons for centralised operations. Industries where communications and access to information are vital can now operate successfully in a distributed manner. With the provision of telecommunications equipment and terminal links, people can communicate freely with their colleagues and access information directly from their homes. The technology allows the possibility of a return to the home office.... For many skilled people, home working provides a freedom and flexibility in line with their expectations and needs. Women may be the prime beneficiaries of home-based working conditions for the obvious reasons. But increasingly, home-working is seen as a genuine option providing more freedom and also more job responsibility.... The uncertainty caued by recession and technological changes in today's world means that industry must be as lean and adaptable as possible to remain competitive. Self employed home based workers are one solution to this problem.

F International employs men as well as women, though in smaller numbers. Other organizations are beginning to experiment with home employment. The same article mentions that 'Rank Xerox have introduced a pilot scheme to make some of their workers home based and ICL have for many years employed off-site technical authors and programmers'. Most of the initial schemes will involve computer professionals, as they will be able to make use of the telecommunications facilities most easily. However, these facilities are improving fast and becoming available even on cheap home computers. Soon such skills and facilities will be in the hands of as many people as require and can make use of them, in many occupations other than

*March 1984

programming and data processing.

We are unlikely to return to a pre-industrial situation but, although the only way forward is on, we may be able to re-create some of the aspects of work that existed before the nineteenth century and develop a pattern of life that is nearer to that of man's previous history than it is to the last two centuries. The mixture may be better than either of the two extremes of working wholly at home or wholly away from home. Either of these can develop its own tyranny. Many women wish for a chance to get out of the home but they are often prevented from taking such a chance because of the inflexibility of the system. Similarly, many men would be glad of some time at home but value the work place, colleagues and the interchange of ideas and information. The importance of this may be more than the simple target of satisfying women who wish to work; it is becoming increasingly difficult for families to sustain a reasonable standard of living on a single income. As in the pre-industrial days, if we are to support the institution of the family at the standard to which we wish it to be accustomed, then it is necessary to make it possible for more of its members – for instance the mother – to contribute to its financial well-being. Gloria Scott, talking in *The Guardian*\* about projects in the Third World, points out that to consider the contribution and needs of women in these schemes has nothing to do with feminism as such: 'It's not a rights issue, but an efficiency one.' This is because much of the crucial work is done by women. The Third World should not be seen simply as a disaster model; we have much to learn as well as to teach.

### F International

For several years people said that we were on the brink of a technological revolution that would cause a complete change in working patterns and the organization of society. Work would be shared out in smaller blocks, so that everyone would have more free time; more and more work would be carried out from home rather than from the place of work; technology would work for us, not we for it. This has signally failed to come about, except in one small corner where a large group of women, led in the first instance by an inspired entrepreneur, have set to and made a life for themselves according to these principles. Far from trying to turn the clock back, as many ecological or communal experiments seem to do, these women have organized a way of living and working that could be a blueprint for future social and occupational change, while making use of every advance in technology.

It is worth quoting the example of F International at this stage in the discussion of issues, as it illustrates the way in which a group of women have actually demonstrated new ways of working to the rest of society, which merely discusses them. Examples of individual women working on their own are given in Chapters 7-9.

\*7 February 1984

F International was founded as Freelance Programmers Limited by Mrs Steve Shirley. The majority of its workers are women and work from home (not always *at* home, however). There are now more than 800 workers and the company is widely known and used by such clients as Ministry of Defence establishments, Bird's Eye Walls, the Forward Trust Group and British Aerospace. Eighty per cent of current customers have come back for more. There are three foreign subsidiaries, including one in New York, but I shall discuss only the parent company here.

Founded in 1962 with a starting group of four workers plus Mrs Shirley, the organization had expanded to eight by 1966. There was a leap to 100 staff in 1967, and by 1975 there were 400. Now there are approximately 800. In 1976 Mrs Shirley was elected as the only woman serving on the Council of the British Computer Society and in 1980 she received an OBE. Mrs Alison Newell is now Chief Executive Officer (UK) and is also President of the Computing Services Association; her photograph is to be seen in the computing newspapers with amazing regularity and she was invited to make a statement to the Confederation of British Industries' Annual Conference in Glasgow in November 1983.

This has to be accounted a success story and it is interesting now to look at the ingredients, since it is uncommon in content as well as in result. Although there are some full-time workers, the majority of the 800 members work both part time and from home. There are some permanent staff (25 per cent) who run the organization; of these, 18 per cent, or 5.75 per cent of the total workers, are both full time and office based. Another 4.5 per cent are full time but home based. The rest are both part time and home based, and all the panel workers are part time and home based. Turning it around, this means that if we count all staff and all panel workers who are part time and home based, they add up to 88 per cent of the whole. Another 2 per cent are part time and office based, which leaves only 10 per cent carrying out a British standard working day.

The panel workers are the freelance workers whose names are kept on a panel to be called upon when needed to fill the requirements of projects for which F International has gained the contract. They can be of either sex, but the majority are women. They must be available for at least twenty hours per week – the minimum 'useful' week – and they must have had at least four years' experience working with computers. They must also be available for a minimum of two working days in each week to work away from home – not in an ordinary office but a client's site. They are therefore a different and more professional group than those for whom I write this book, but they serve as an example of how such an organization can work. Panel workers are entitled to vary the amounts of time for which they are available and may also indicate periods when they do not wish to work at all, such as school holidays. Time off for school nativity plays – the bugbear of the working parent – is run of the mill at F International, and freelance means freelance: they may work for other employers whenever they wish.

In spite of this freedom, a high proportion of panel workers have stayed with F International for many years, and the formula clearly works: 33.8 per cent have been with the group for more than five years and there are a number who have received the Ten Year Award (twenty-one in 1983-4). Panel workers are not usually unemployed: 75 per cent of those available currently have work.

The company turnover was just short of £5 million in the year 1982-3. The services provided are no longer simply programming, but include specialists in a range of software and systems services, such as analysts, programmers, systems designers, specification writers and consultants in expert systems, insurance work and so forth. There is also a micro service for advising clients and tailoring systems for businesses with a turnover of less than £5 million.

The principles that the company follows are, first, that the ideal structure for both client and worker is a mixture of home- and out-work. This is why it is described as working *from* home, rather than *at* home. The advantages to the clients of this insistence on some time spent on site are that they can get to know the people who are working for them, check on progress of work in hand and get a feeling for whether it is running to schedule. The advantage to workers is that it gets them out and about and prevents them from becoming isolated or remote. The tyranny of the home can become as oppressive as the tyranny of the office if there are no provisions for working out, and also workers can become out of date and lose touch with modern developments.

The second important principle, stemming from the difficult task created by offering the flexibility of the first, is that none of this can work without effective management. Effective management in this case means a very different brand from that usually met with in companies. They call it 'home grown' since methods have had to be evolved to cope with the complex structure of the organization. The ideas may be similar to those of management in other well-run companies, but the rigour with which they are applied is different.

The company has a managing director and five regional offices, each with a regional manager, and a head office with five divisions (administration, business development, finance, personnel and technical services). Each regional manager has a substructure of managers to cope with administration and sales support, including sales, estimating, managing resources (the staffing of projects) and handling the separate client accounts. Project managers work to these managers and they themselves manage the technical panel – the workers in the field. The challenges for the workforce are described as: specification, liaison and management of projects.

The unit of work is the project, which is defined as a specific piece of work done under contract to a client. A set procedure is followed. The work is first discussed with a client by salaried staff from F International; a proposal is defined; a project manager is assigned; next a team of workers (taken from the panel and paid on an hourly rate) is appointed. The project is carried out, a review held and feedback provided. Estimates are checked against actual costs and an analysis is undertaken of any variation and its cause. The contract is between F International and the client, and the workers are contracted to F International, not to the client, and are paid an hourly rate. This provides security and stability for all parties to a contract.

One of the tightest areas is the estimating of costs, and F International reckon that they have got this – probably the most difficult task in providing any kind of computing service – down to a fine art. During a project the workers report at least once a week to their project manager. She reports equally often to the client account manager and the regional manager. Management is therefore one of the biggest overheads of the company, but it is the crux of the whole business, and the success in this area is probably the cause of the success of the company as a whole.

We know that women make good programmers and analysts, that part-time workers give good value for money and that companies are glad to contract out work of this kind for which they do not in the current economic climate wish to retain full-time staff. It has not previously been clear that women make good managers, because although there are some excellent women managers they are few in number and could be atypical. Here we have an example of a successful company run on unusual lines by women for women and providing an example of good management which is not passing unnoticed in the traditional male-dominated companies. It seems to illustrate quite clearly that women have something special to contribute to management skills as well as to the field of computing in general.

It would be even more interesting to know how this company has succeeded in finding so many women both capable of and willing to be managers. I think that the answer lies in the fact that F International, founded by a woman understanding the average woman's problems, met women on their own terms and was therefore able to draw on resources and extract contributions from women which they are often unwilling to provide. It is, as Gloria Scott says, not so much a question of rights as of efficiency to consider the needs and characteristics of female workers. There is an unusually high proportion of managers in the company because of its peculiar problems, and the majority of these work part time and from home. This would be unthinkable in a normal company and yet it manifestly works, reinforcing the impression that the major obstacle to this kind of structure is usually hidebound thinking.

F International uses mainly women because it is they who apply for this work. Ninety-five per cent have children and the age structure of the company shows that the majority (approximately 70 per cent) are aged between thirty and forty, the age at which their children are likely to be dependent though not still babes in arms. However, there is no reason why men should not follow a similar work pattern, as it has proved to be so effective in practice. F International makes money and clients are satisfied to the point of commenting favourably on the speed and efficiency of the part-time workers and coming back for more. We are not talking about just a few special or dedicated women, but about 800 workers. They cannot be so very far from a normal distribution of the professional population, even if they are self-selected and following an unusual pattern. Thus it seems that they could be providing a feasibility study of the much-heralded, but as yet scarcely to be observed, change in working patterns as the result of the developments in technology. I am not suggesting a sweeping away of offices and traditional work places, and nor are F International. The value of meeting together and the need for certain services to be centralized means that a return to pre-industrial conditions is not to be contemplated. However, we can grow and adapt, changing as we do and providing more and varied occupations for more people as we do. Women have the greatest need for these changes and can therefore effect them first and provide an example to the rest of society.

*Part II*

# Some Ideas and Practical Examples

# Introduction

The first two chapters in this part give some suggestions for activities for which computers based in the home might be useful. Where possible these are linked with the personal case histories given in the succeeding chapters. These are the stories of individual women who have, for one reason or another, become involved with computers and have made a successful career of computing.

The first three have created businesses which they run from home; two of them are university educated (the third left school at sixteen) and all three are middle-class and middle-aged. Since to have taken up computing at least three years ago and to have enough money to purchase the necessary equipment presupposes both education and social privilege, this is almost inevitable. The second group of women, all university educated but not all middle-aged, have entered the computer industry itself and earn salaries. The third group have computers at home and do not use them as a source of income, although one of them is preparing for a return to work when her child is a little older. One has professional qualifications and the other left school at sixteen with no qualifications.

*Chapter 5*

# Possible Applications for the Micro at Home (1)*

In this chapter and the next I shall look at uses to which a microcomputer could be put by someone working at home. There are many traditional women's jobs where computers are coming to play an important role, and a knowledge of how to use them would be both useful and an aid in the competitive job market. Nursing is an example which leaps immediately to mind, as nurses are beginning to use computers for administrative and clerical tasks, in the wards for what we call 'remote data capture' – collecting information away from the site of the large computer using a small hand held variety – and in all kinds of complex medical and laboratory equipment. Banks, traditionally large employers of women, use computers; computers are beginning to replace cash registers in shops and point-of-sale sites traditionally manned by women.

Teaching is an area in which the ability to use a computer and teach others is a trump card in the careers game at the moment and will become an essential requirement very soon. The need for teachers who know even a little about computers is particularly desperate in Britain where the government has made a gesture towards providing equipment but has not preceded this by sufficient special training for teachers. This surely is an opportunity for women to start influencing things by helping their pupils to

---

*All prices quoted in this chapter and the next are subject to change and do not include VAT.

develop reasonable computer behaviour as well as skills. The field is given to men by default, but they really need the help of women in order to do it well; on the other hand, women need an area in which they can operate as other than second-class citizens.

It is sensible, therefore, to become familiar with computers even if you intend a full-time away-from-home career. However, the examples given here are confined to those activities that can be carried on at home, as this is perhaps the area of greatest ignorance and greatest need.

Most of the microcomputers advertised in newspapers or on television, and most of those to be found in people's homes, are of the variety known as 'home computers'. These are cheap and, while they are not to be despised as a means of becoming acquainted with some of the concepts central to an understanding of computers, they are not usually adequate for anyone who wants to earn a living with computers. It is sometimes possible to start with such a computer and gradually develop, purchasing more expensive equipment as you can afford it, but care is needed because it is also possible to waste a lot of money if this approach does not work and you have to start again with a better computer. Chapter 12 describes the differences, both in price and performance, between what are referred to as home computers, desk-top (or business) computers, and the various types of portable computer which fall between the other two categories in both characteristics.

It is only fair to say of these little home computers that, although they are not in general useful for complex tasks, it is possible to do amazing things with them. It is not easy, however, and you can waste time trying. If you are going to give yourself a reasonable chance of developing your skill with computers to the point where you can earn money or provide yourself with some substantially useful service, you should give yourself a good start and think in terms of something more powerful.

Let us first look at what might be a useful application. The word 'application' is used in the context of computers to refer to an activity or task to which the general-purpose tool, the computer, can be applied with good effect. Managing company accounts, running membership lists of a voluntary organization, handling and laying out large quantities of text, preparing indexes for books and catalogues for small libraries or record collections are all tasks suitable for computerization, and therefore are applications for which programs, known under the generic name of 'application software', can be written.

### Home typing and word processing

Many women have worked in offices, in clerical positions of higher or lower degree, and so if for some reason they find themselves looking for work that they can do at home, home typing is an obvious solution. A good typewriter is quite expensive but can usually be justified by the expected returns. There is always a lot of work for good typists to do in this way, particularly at the moment when offices are careful not to to be over-staffed and therefore often find themselves under-staffed at peak periods or during the holiday season. They often therefore need a list of reliable home typists to call upon in time of need.

Home typing, by definition, is likely to involve longish documents, reports and even books. A company's day-to-day correspondence is usually coped with by staff on the premises and it is only the occasional longer documents, needed at irregular intervals and then usually in a hurry, that are farmed out. How much more suitable for this is a word-processing package on a microcomputer than a typewriter. Word processing does not offer much benefit for short documents to a fast, accurate typist, but everyone benefits enormously, whatever the level of typing skill, if the document is either long or, in the case of a draft, likely to be altered. Another advantage of word processing is that the typist does not even need to be very fast or accurate, as corrections are easy to make and the whole process is speeded up by being computerized. It is therefore a good opening for someone with moderate typing skills and an eye for layout and document design.

Anyone who is familiar with the characteristics of a word processor will be aware that it offers the opportunity to make corrections to text without extensive re-typing; it allows the moving around of blocks of text from one part of a document to another – from one chapter of a report to another, if necessary, as well as from one paragraph or page to another. Large new chunks of text can be inserted and misspellings rectified; the previous text will just be shunted forward to make room.

As well as these major advantages, a word processor (or a microcomputer using applications software for word processing) also offers lesser benefits. The actual entry of text is nearly always faster than on a typewriter once you have mastered the small variations on the keyboard. Computer keyboards are in theory identical to typewriter keyboards – at least those on desk-top computers; this is another difference between home and business equipment – but, because there are a few extra keys for the computing functions, the home keys sometimes feel as if they are slightly displaced from the accustomed position. The quality of the keys and the touch also varies, and some keyboards cannot accept the letters as fast as the fastest typist can type. These things are improving all the time, but if you cannot afford the best quality it is nonetheless generally found that, even if your keystrokes are a little slower than on a typewriter, your rate of entry is faster because you never have to worry about an end of line or carriage return: the computer calculates when it has reached an end of line and itself swings around to a new line and 'wraps' the word so as not to break it in the middle.

Another considerable advantage is the comparative silence of a word processor. The printers that come with computers are very noisy, but since the text is entered first into the computer and only later, at your convenience, printed out, the noisy part can be executed at an appropriate moment.

Mothers who try to cram in a little home work in the evenings after the children have gone to bed can therefore do so without disturbing anyone else.

As well as enabling them to work at home, a computer can help to prevent the 'de-skilling' of women. The majority of women marry and the majority of them have children. Most mothers choose to break their careers for a period and any work they do at home is usually low skilled. One of the examples given later in the book is of a woman who, before she had children, was personal assistant to the administrator of an opera house – a job of immense variety and interest, and one at a level that involved very little actual typing, as there were people lower in the hierarchy to do that. When she needed occupation and money while tied to the home, she began to take in home typing. Although the work was often quite complicated – documents for lawyers and so forth – it was work that she would have scorned when in full-time employment. After a year or two of this she turned to computing and, although she continued to do much of the same work, it was infinitely more interesting. This is because using a computer is interesting in itself; it allows concentration on the skilled part of the work, it allows the development of new kinds of work and, finally, the 'throughput' is so much greater that the financial rewards increase to the point where it is possible to decide to do less work, hire assistants or to live better than anticipated on the proceeds of your own industry.

### Practical suggestions

*Equipment.* To carry out word processing commercially involves the purchase of expensive equipment. The very minimum would be a cheap business computer with word-processing software plus a cheap, slow daisy wheel printer. The cheapest configuration at the moment is the Wren Executive, which comes with software included at £1000, and a Juki printer (approx. £399) or a Brother (approx. £445). If more money is available, it would best be spent on a faster printer (e.g. Ricoh Flowriter at £1695) and a sheet feeder (approx. £480).

Although word processing can be learned with a home computer, it cannot be carried out commercially without a business system. For this reason word processing is one of the most expensive ways to start in computing. There are dozens of computers, and dozens of word-processing packages, which would do the job. Go for a machine with standard operating system (CP/M* or MSDOS) and well-known word-processing software, such as WordStar, Perfect Writer, Peachtext, the Word, Superwriter or another market-leading brand name.

If finance is tight, perhaps a local group of women could join together to purchase the equipment and work out a shift system of using it to fit in with

*CP/M is the trade mark of Digital Research Inc.

other commitments.

*Charges.* These change from month to month. At the moment, if you do a good, accurate job, and work quickly, you can charge £10 per hour and undercut all the bureaus, who have to charge enough to cover overheads and take a commission on work. A home typist may charge no more than £5 per hour for the same work, so it is necessary to work twice as fast on a word processor as on a typewriter to justify the charge. This should be possible. (See the example of Kate in Chapter 7.)

### Indexing books

One of the more interesting activities that can be developed alongside word processing, or carried on as a single occupation in its own right, is professional book indexing. Indexing is a skilled profession and it is certainly not the case that anyone with a knowledge of typing could index a book. However, as with any other profession, it can be learned. The skill lies in the judgement of what items are worth indexing and exactly how they should be entered into an index. There is at least one program (see Chapter 7) that incorporates nearly all the principles and aids to book indexing and enables the task to be carried out on a computer.

A good index is not simply a list of words and page numbers. It should attach details and ideas to the words and provide for cross-referencing of an intelligent kind. If I look up a subject like 'Factory Reform' in a book on social and economic history, I find the entry:

Factory Reform – see Reform

Under Reform I find:

Reform
    associations, 81
    clubs, 81
    factory, 124 – 126, 349, 455 – 64, 470
    land, 391 – 392
    *see also* Acts of Parliament *and* various trades

The indexing program not only stores all entries on a disk, sorts into alphabetical order and lays out according to BSI rules, but also allows for publishers' house style and provides all kinds of special aids to the indexer. These include a key press for cross-referencing, so that an entry under 'Factory Reform' will also be entered under 'Reform, factory' as well as simple 'Reform' or simple 'Factory' if desired. A keyword device enables long scientific, medical or otherwise hard-to-spell words or phrases to be stored once into a keyword symbol and subsequently to be called up at a single key press. For instance, 'monosodium glutamate' could be referenced under % and every time you press the % key the words 'monosodium glutamate' will appear on the screen and be entered in the file without your having to type them in.

For someone who is already a professional indexer with regular work, a computer would probably pay for itself in a comparatively short time. For someone who has to learn the indexing techniques and also drum up work, the profits would not be so immediate or certain, but there is a need for indexers who can work quickly and reduce the heavy overheads of manual indexing. It is work that is already done mostly from home by part-time professionals and is an ideal occupation for some of the women currently wishing that they could find paid work to do from home.

Future trends indicate that more and more information will be kept in 'database' form and as the information revolution develops there is going to be a greater demand for computer indexing services of all kinds.

*Practical suggestions*

There are some programs which do 'automatic' indexing within the word-processor software. Few of these have a good reputation among skilled indexers and the only one that I can recommend is Macrex/Micrex (or Indexer), which costs £75 for the small version (Micrex) and £190 for the large (Macrex). It will run on any computer that uses the CP/M operating system and has 48K of RAM available. One of the cheapest of these is the Wren or, alternatively, although only able to run the smaller Micrex program, the Epson PX-8, which has the advantage of being battery operated and portable as well as being no larger than an A4 piece of paper (approx. £850). For either machine, you would, of course, need a printer. The PX-8 has a portable 40-column printer (approx. £150) and the Wren can use any printer. A cheap option is the Epson RX80 at £278. (See also the example of Drusilla in Chapter 7.)

## Research

This sounds like a dangerous course to recommend to the beginner computer-user. However, much of the numerical data that people use to back up hypotheses and descriptive research is the result of very crude number crunching. If you wish to learn to program at all you can very quickly get yourself into the position where you can perform simple number counts – frequencies or distributions – and more complex counts – cross-tabulations or frequencies of a combination of characteristics. Laying it out to look like the Statistical Package for the Social Services is another matter, but you can cheat and do that part by hand if necessary.

Many professional women turn to research as a desirable activity during the years when they need to work part time and partly from home. Many organizations cannot afford to employ research workers on a regular basis, but can get budgets for separate projects on an irregular basis. Still more organizations regularly collect information and statistics which they never analyse because they have not the time or in-house skills to do so. There are, in fact, excellent packages available on micros, developed for the sole purpose of carrying out research work – analysing and also collecting data and planning interview schedules. They are not the cheapest type of software, because presented in a sophisticated form this kind of thing is costly to write. As professional tools for anyone who can see their way to earning money with them, they are well worth their purchase price, particularly as they can be set off against tax by a self-employed person.

*Practical suggestions*
The chapter on F International (Chapter 4) shows the way in which the organization of work may develop to allow this kind of work to be done at home using a microcomputer or a terminal to a larger machine. It is difficult to give precise recommendations at the moment, as any venture in this direction is likely to be pioneering. However, there are numerous examples of medium- and small-sized research organizations that are struggling to learn the skills of microcomputing to enable them to perform their customary tasks of data analysis on micros in the office. The situation is similar to that of home typing, where the offer of a good freelance service would cause the companies to sigh with relief, put down the manuals and hand over the work.

If you already work for such an organization and would rather work from home, then the equipment to purchase is a good business system with adequate disk-storage space. This would have to be something like a Sirius with disks that hold enough data (cost about £2500) or a cheaper system capable of taking a Winchester disk. The Epson QX-10 at £1735 plus £1500 for the Winchester, or the IBM at approximately £2500 plus £1500 for a Winchester, or the Wren at £1000 plus £1500 for a Winchester, are all possibilities. A Winchester disk is a particularly nice thing to have, though very expensive, because it enormously increases the speed of each operation and also makes it unnecessary to keep on changing disks.

The various prices quoted above show quite clearly that this is not a cheap activity. The software is also expensive. You need either a database (e.g. dBASE II at £435) or a survey analysis program (SNAP at £650 or Microsurvey at £1200).

There is a group called the Study Group for the Use of Computers in Survey Analysis (Chairman: Hugh Neffendorf, MVA Systematica, 112 Strand, London WC1) from which further information and advice can be obtained.

## Voluntary work

Many people, both male and female, put their time and skills at the disposal of charitable bodies, social clubs, self-help groups and other such organizations. There is usually, by definition, a shortage of money and a shortage of labour-saving equipment. Much of the work involves membership lists, newsletters, accounts, money-raising activities and so on. A computer is a significant aid in nearly all these areas. Membership lists, newsletters and envelope addressing can be catered for by a word-processing/mailing package. Accounts can be handled by a database program or a simple accounting package, or, if the organization is not large and complex, by a program written by you for the purpose. Other activities, like an analysis of membership by activity and response, could be carried out. More effective fund raising could be assisted by this kind of analysis and newsletters or appeals targeted to the most appropriate or demonstrably responsive section of the membership or wider population.

If you are learning as you go, you will not work a miracle overnight, but there would be a double benefit from trying. The first is a charitable contribution and the second is an opportunity to learn by tackling a real problem. The dispiriting thing about computers is that the effort involved in mastering them is very considerable and for many people it is difficult to summon up sufficient energy except for a purpose that is patently worth achieving and not simply a practice exercise.

### Practical suggestions

If you plan to set up a sophisticated service offering word-processing and mailing facilities, it may be necessary to purchase the more expensive types of equipment. However, this is one area where it is possible to achieve a lot with inexpensive kit. With ingenuity and diligence a very great deal can be done on a home computer. The financial forecasting of a national charity, for example, has been carried out on a ZX81 costing £75. The estimating of book costs for a well-known publishing house has been done on a similar machine. The ZX81 has been superseded now by the Spectrum (£125), which is much more powerful, and if the Sinclair QL performs up to expectation there will be very considerable computing power available for under £500. Other machines, like the BBC and the Commodore 64, are relatively cheap and capable of much in the right hands.

*Chapter 6*

# Possible Applications for the Micro at Home (2)

### Programming

I have referred several times in passing to programming as a possible use for a personal computer. To become a professional programmer requires training and experience, but a little knowledge of programming, and in particular a familiarity with the basic concepts, is invaluable at all levels of using a computer and in many other ways as well. Programming at this level is something that you can quite well teach yourself from a book, although to clarify some points you may occasionally find it useful to consult someone who has experience in writing a program and getting it to run on a microcomputer.

The uses of programming are manifold. Even if you never manage to write a program that does anything to repay you for the effort you put into writing it, you will have gained important insights into how the computer itself approaches problems. This, contrary to popular misconception, while not an indispensable preliminary to using a computer as a general tool, will enormously speed up the task of mastering its use for purposes other than programming – for all the other activities described here and under the heading of applications. The kind of mistakes that people make are very understandable in the light of their general ignorance of how computers work, and quite inexplicable to anyone who has the slightest familiarity with the logic of the system. Thus, although all measures that make computers easier for the general public to use are worthwhile, it is probably also true that the general public should itself make a slightly greater effort. The power and versatility of computers can only be diminished if they have to be reduced to the lowest common denominator for permanently rather than temporarily 'naïve' users. Perhaps women could show the way here, since they often have more time to devote to further education and training.

Apart from preparation for more computing of a different kind, programming is also one of the best forms of mind-sharpening exercise. Sometimes with our obsession with physical fitness – as an idea, anyway – I wonder whether the *mens sana* idea has been forgotten in the pursuit of *corpus sanus*. Women who have been relatively confined by domesticity for some time are often worried about being woolly minded and here is an excellent opportunity for them to kill two birds with one stone – tone up their minds and acquire a new skill.

The best way to learn to program is to write a program yourself and apply it to some practical task, following through every stage: entering the data, accessing it, manipulating it and reporting back the results. It can be a slow and painful process to begin with, but it is a good way to learn and wonderfully stimulating and satisfying. It also makes you a better judge of a program than if you had never written anything more than play routines yourself and, for anyone who goes on to make their living from criticizing and evaluating other people's programs, it is an invaluable training.

Some people might continue along the programming line, and once they have perfected their skills and gained further experience, earn a living that way. There will be other people, like those who work for F International described in Chapter 4, who are already qualified programmers and will want to work at home, using their computer both as a stand-alone device on which to write and develop programs and also as a terminal to a larger machine. In this way they can work as out-workers to a larger organization. It can, however, be difficult to come into pure programming late in life; it is hard to beat the young at that game, as their brains are sharper and their educational groundwork is better. Moreover, there are plenty of young brilliant programmers, but a grave shortage of people who can combine some programming skills and an understanding of computers with the experience and judgement that come with age.

This slightly cautious approach applies mostly to the traditional area of applications programming, which involves writing database management programs, accounts packages and so forth. In fact, these days there are areas where less elaborate programming skills are nonetheless valuable. Some of the software houses that write programs for home computers – Acornsoft for the BBC and Acorn computers, Island Logic and others – are waking up to the fact that women form 50 per cent of the market and are trying to produce software attractive to girls at the educational level and women at the adult level. The results so far are pretty derisory and include such things as marriage guidance, recipe books and other offensive titles. What better authors and originators of software for women than women themselves? Although programs on the level of Cindy dolls for girls would serve to encourage the current stereotyping of gender, there are other areas of female interest and also aspects of activities appealing to boys which also appeal to girls. Girls may not enjoy killer-driller games as much as boys, but that does not prevent them liking games of strategy and the modern fantasy games – 'Dungeons and Dragons' and so forth – particularly if the subject matter is not entirely male dominated. There is no reason why horse racing or games of equestrian skill should not be dramatized on home computers as well as car racing: they are just as exciting and appeal to girls as well as boys.

Things are improving a bit, but not enough, and it is partly because men, however good their intentions, are not good at thinking up the right subjects. Nearly all programming in the educational field, particularly that done freelance by teachers, is carried out by men. Virginia Makins, of *The Times Educational Supplement*, wrote 'Basically it is a male preserve. Conferences are full of hollow-eyed young men in their late 20s pressing flysheets about their latest bit of cottage-industry software into your hands'. The women teachers who have interested themselves in computing have not only been able to contribute a lot; they have often achieved quicker promotion than would otherwise have been likely. So learn to program and sell your skills to a software house. Or, alternatively, get involved with your local school and help to change the emphasis and presentation of computers in education. Some schools are nervous of letting parents in as voluntary helpers, often for good reason, but they will surely not refuse free gifts of programs as they are desperately short of good material and cannot pay commercial prices. Once you have discovered that your programs are useful and stand the test of being used in class, you can think about selling them commercially and will be able to quote the fact that they are already being used in schools. Alternatively, if they are not good enough, then you can set to work to improve your skills.

This advice is not quite as easy to follow as I imply because programs of this kind are often what we call machine-dependent – i.e. they will only run on the kind of machine for which they have been written. With a little care they can be made adaptable, but this is another reason for thinking out quite carefully what you want to do, which market you wish to enter, and then choosing the equipment with such details in mind.

*Practical suggestions*
It is possible to teach yourself to program in most computer languages if you can get hold of a good book. BASIC is provided on all home computers, and so this is the cheapest one for starters. There is a continuing debate as to whether it is a good programming language or not, but it is true to say that many useful programs are written in BASIC, that many computers allow only BASIC or machine code and that it is possible to learn the rudiments of

programming as well in BASIC as in most other languages.

A Commodore 64 computer with free BASIC provided costs approximately £200. The BBC machine costs approximately £300. These are both tape-based computers in their basic form, though both can have disk drives attached. A portable machine like the Epson HX20 or the PX-8, or the Tandy or NEC version of a similar computer, offer a chance to learn to program for a different kind of application. A disk-based machine will inevitably cost more – from £700 to over £2000, according to what you choose. On a disk-based machine you have a much greater choice of computer languages. The computers that use the CPM operating system have the widest choice, as almost every known language is available on them. Pascal is a good language, as is C language. The more modern trend towards artificial intelligence has made languages like LISP and Microprolog popular, and if I were starting afresh I think I would choose one of these.

You cannot really expect to launch yourself as a professional programmer without some work experience and in-service training. In that case the language and equipment will be dictated by the firm that you work for. (See Chapter 4 on F International for an illustration; see also the examples of Rose, Mary and Christine in Chapters 7-9.)

The following books on programming are recommended:
*30 Hour BASIC*, National Extension College
*Elementary BASIC and Elementary Pascal*, Ledgard and Singer, Fontana
*A Practical Introduction to Pascal* (revised edition), Wilson and Addyman, Macmillan
*Principles of Programming with FORTRAN*, E B James, Pitman
*The C Programming Language*, Kernighan and Ritchie, Addison Wesley
*Software Tools in Pascal*, Kernighan and Plauger, Addison Wesley
*Elements of Programming Style*, Kernighan and Plauger, Addison Wesley

### Training and consultancy

More than one of the examples in the following three chapters of women who have made something from nothing out of computing illustrate the fact that there is a grave shortage of people to teach and train the rest. Training in particular is an area where part-time women with specialized skills can be useful. There are literally thousands, if not millions, of workers already in jobs who need to be trained in word processing and other computing skills and who cannot be spared by their firms to go on courses. They have to be trained fast and on-site. What better than a part-time, flexible, self-taught expert to fill such a gap? Someone, moreover, who has probably done the job before it was computerized; has learned the new skills the hard way and is aware of the problems that the average person has in coming to terms with computing, who is not interested in the intricacies or clever features of the machine, or why it does what it does, but sees as the prime target the understanding of what it can do and how to make it do that with least disruption of present methods.

Training clients, particularly in the use of word-processing packages, database management programs, accounts packages, financial modelling, is useful and, with a little thought and planning, not difficult. More difficult but equally valuable is the help and advice that comes under the heading of consultancy. A wider knowledge is required of hardware, software and the nature of the business that is to be computerized. However, the general level of despair and ignorance in the population as a whole is such that, as long as false claims are not made and limits of expertise are clearly defined, there is also a role for limited advice and guidance even by non-professionals. It is being offered all over the place by people, both professional and amateur, who know less than they should and, although in an ideal world advice of this kind should be strictly licensed and limited, life is very far from ideal and help is needed everywhere. There is certainly a role for people to impart their experience to others, particularly at a time when the official professionals often come from a part of the computer market which is in practice very different from the micro market. The experts from large computer departments often know very little about desk-top machines, but because they are members of the British Computer Society their advice is sought and taken. Customers on the new frontiers of technology are starved of good advice. Women who are practical in their approach to the subject, good at understanding the clients' needs and able to communicate effectively can provide a useful service of this kind, provided the project is limited in scope and the client properly involved in decision-making.

*Practical suggestions*

Before you can join a national training network such as that organized by CIRCUIT UK for word processing, or be on the books of a national organization like the Information and Word Processing Association, it is necessary to have formal training and qualifications as a trainer. However, the dearth of people who know about computers and, in particular, the electronic office type of application, is so great that it is quite possible to go it alone without formal qualifications. This kind of statement shocks professional bodies, but provided that you set your own high standards, and given that the business that you are likely to get will come by word of mouth and personal recommendation, then there is a sort of self-regulating method. When no formal training in these kinds of skills exists and when there is a shortage of qualified people, then the self-made, self-appointed specialist is bound to grow up. For many people it can be a good idea to learn on the job, and charge little or nothing for the first few pieces of work in order to compensate the customer for any initial semi-competence. Thus one gets the necessary practical experience without feeling a fraud. (See also the examples of Kate and Rose in Chapters 7 and 8.)

## Accounts

There are two levels at which computers can be used for accounting. One is the traditional task of book keeping, and this does not require accounting skills. Book keeping covers the routine tasks of entering details of sales and invoices into one ledger, purchases into another and perhaps keeping control of stock in and required in another. The three tasks can be kept entirely separate, or alternatively stock and sales can be linked in order to keep a good balance. Book keeping is not always easy to learn, as the example later in this book illustrates, and for many people the terms and methods are unfamiliar and incomprehensible at first. However, it has traditionally been done by people without professional training and is not beyond anyone with determination and average intelligence.

The next stage, represented in computerized accounting systems by the nominal ledger, involves either some knowledge of accountancy or working in co-operation with the company accountants. The entering of information into this ledger can be done by someone who is not an accountant, but the ledger must first be 'set up' by someone with accounting skills, or else the result might be disastrous. With proper care, however, this stage can also be learned and then carried out on behalf of companies who do not wish to employ a full-time person to do the work. Alternatively, the person who has taken the trouble to learn how to run a computerized accounts system can set it up for a firm and train one of their employees to operate it with back-up and advice from her as and when necessary.

*Practical suggestions*
It is probably best to take a course in book keeping if you know nothing about accounts (as Christine in the examples in Chapter 9 has done). Home computers such as the Commodore 64 have very good, if unsophisticated, accounting software available for them at a moderate price (approx. £50). This kind of accounting package is quite adequate for a small business, perhaps a one-man business or one with a few large rather than many small customers. Although quite unsuitable for businesses of any size, this software and machine could provide a basis of training in accounting for you and could service the myriad very small businesses that have always existed and which are increasing in number in the current economic climate. They are, by definition, the kinds of firm that will not particularly wish to spend several thousand pounds computerizing their own accounts and will be glad to farm the work out.

The alternative is to invest several thousand pounds in a business machine, printer and more sophisticated ledger software. Almost any business microcomputer with printer (price from £1500 to £3500) can run the better-known accounting packages, of which Peachtree, TABS and Pulsar are perhaps the market leaders. All these provide training opportunities to customers at a price. (See also the example of Nora in Chapter 7.)

## Sales

Women make good salespeople and some, though not by any means all, computer firms and dealers send people out to try to get sales. Certainly it is something that customers expect. Some companies do not find it cost effective in general and only do it for potentially large orders, but a visit to the site bearing equipment and programs to demonstrate is something that can be done on a part-time basis and also from home. It is not necessarily ideal in the thinking of traditional firms, but times are changing and new formulae are needed to solve the problems of survival in the modern world. Knowledge-able women, who have a good regular contact with a firm and whose time does not have to be charged out at the normal £25 or £30 per hour of an employee incurring the standard overheads, can be a valuable asset to a small- to medium-sized business.

*Practical suggestions*

An article in *Computing*\* bemoans the serious shortage of computer salespeople. The writer is concerned with the high-flying salesmen who work for large computer companies, but small firms are feeling the shortage as well. To sell computers requires a certain amount of technical knowledge and also, ideally, some training in the art of selling. A firm is more likely to take on a trainee salesperson who already knows about computers than someone who needs training in both areas. It is therefore worth considering training courses in computing and perhaps also in sales techniques. One of the TOPS courses listed in the guide for London is entitled 'Micro Systems Sales and Marketing', another is 'Information Technology and Salesmanship' while a third is 'Microcomputer Sales Staff'. The first requires A-level, the second O-level in at least English and mathematics, and the third requires previous business or industrial experience as well as education to O-level. (See also the examples of Rose and Sarah in Chapter 8.)

## Journalism

Advertisements appear quite regularly in the computer press for computer journalists, and you do not have to know much about computing to become one. The standard of writing in the better computer papers is astonishingly high in journalistic terms, but there are many levels and everyone must begin somewhere. If you have any kind of writing ability and even a beginner's knowledge of computing you can get started and learn as you go. Try to get hold of copies of the trade papers and find the advertisements, or approach any one of the literally hundreds of micro magazines that are being spawned at the moment. The shelves of W.H. Smith will give you some names and ideas. The book-publishing world is getting somewhat flooded at the moment, but publishing houses are always looking for good titles and anyone with a good idea stands a fair chance.

\*March 1984

*Practical suggestions*

Get hold of some professional computer papers, read the advertisements and see what is required. You will obviously need to know a little about computers, but a familiarity with the jargon, an interest in the subject and the usual requirements of journalism are probably sufficient qualifications for you to have a fair chance of getting started.

## Specialist databases

One or two people have had the idea of compiling information about specialist subjects and making themselves known as a source. One example is for people who collect antiques. This is a very popular hobby but hunting down an item is often a difficult and long-drawn-out affair. One woman has therefore had the idea of gathering together a file of information, a database, on a home computer in order to provide a central source for such enthusiasts. There are many subjects, like compiling and combining lists from antiquarian booksellers, for which the same would be useful. Similarly, running or working as part of an antique-book business is very suitable work for anyone with a computer. At the moment it tends to be a small, rather in-group kind of subject whose afficionados know each other or are on the same networks, but there is opportunity to start some service not yet thought of from which you could perhaps later make your fortune. The compiling of information into database systems is a major growth area and there is no reason why the private operator should not set a trend and make a corner for herself before the market is saturated by people anxious to cash in on a new moneyspinner.

*Practical suggestions*

Compiling specialist databases is an occupation that is ideal for starting on a cheap home computer, though it is possible that if the venture takes off you will need to exchange your equipment for something more sophisticated and begin again. The Sinclair QL looks as if it will be perfect for this kind of application (cost £400), but the Spectrum (£125) and the Commodore 64 or the BBC computer are all good choices. If you wish to start out in a more ambitious way, there is the Wren (£1000), or any business machine. Some computers have software 'bundled' (given away free with them) and if you can find one that has a good database then your expenses will be less. The best upmarket database software is dBASE II at £435.

*Courses and books:* The Open University has courses on database theory and practice. There do not seem to be any TOPS courses, but probably in some areas Local Education Authorities or polytechnics will be running suitable courses. There are also books introducing the theory of database management and choice of software for inexperienced users which should be available through your local library or bookshop.* (See also the example of Marjorie in Chapter 9.)

*see Database Primer, R. Deakin, Century 1983

## Summary

Perhaps one depressing fact has now emerged clearly: earning a living with computers, unlike studying or playing with computers, involves a considerable initial outlay. The profits are correspondingly great, but for many people the lack of finance may indicate that they would do better to learn about computers through courses or home computing and then get a paid job that provides the equipment necessary to work on.

*Chapter 7*

# Nora, Drusilla and Kate

Nora Franglen, Drusilla Calvert and Kate Jennings are examples of women who have taught themselves how to use microcomputers and have set up businesses that they run from home.

*Nora*
Nora Franglen's entry into computing provides a very good illustration of one of the computing phrases which mystifies newcomers most completely. The word 'boot', or 'reboot' (also used in the cryptic message 'bootstrap error' which occasionally appears on the screen), is used to indicate starting up the computer from scratch, from the moment of switching on the power. This is a sort of catch-22 situation for the people who write the software that controls the system, because the electronics will not go into action until some instructions have been received. But instructions are needed to get into the instruction-containing part of the system. Therefore, a short piece of code with relevant instructions, to proceed to the next stage, has to be built into the hardware to come into action immediately with the arrival of power from the electric current. Thus it is getting itself up without external help. The parallel was thought to be that of a cowboy getting up from the ground by pushing against some part of his own body, or pulling on his own bootlaces, or bootstraps, to get the leverage to raise his body from the ground after a night of sleeping rough.

This may give you some idea of why computer jargon is hard to follow. The parallels can usually be justified but seem quirky, to say the least, to the average person. Nora turned to computing as a way of getting up with no visible means of external support from where she had fallen after a particular crisis in her life.

She read modern languages at Cambridge and later took a secretarial course, which, although she did not make use of at the time, she has since found invaluable. She next worked in an administrative capacity at the British Council, married and left to have children. She had three children and was a 'non-stop mother' for ten years, after which she decided to look for part-time work, both for financial reasons and because she wanted an occupation. The obvious job for her was translating and as her husband was a biochemist she made a speciality of translating medical and pharmaceutical works. She did this for six years and also took a post-graduate diploma in technical translating and did part-time teaching after qualifying.

This is a picture that is very recognizable to many well-educated modern women: a picture of someone with ability and qualifications and a great deal of energy, but a career that has been fragmented by a preference for motherhood. There emerges a woman of middle age with good starting qualifications and insufficient experience or clout with a particular employer to find a job easily in a world where the only sure way of being employed is keeping the job you have already. She would probably have made her way slowly up through various slightly unsatisfactory jobs to something interesting and sustaining, but would almost certainly have operated below the level of her ability and suffered considerable boredom and frustration as a result.

Then the quiet tenor of Nora's life was shattered by a crisis in her marriage. She felt an urgent need to work outside the home and got a job through a friend in a small firm. One of the most important routine tasks in this firm was the thrice-weekly production of a news bulletin. Nora started to edit the bulletin and quickly found that the administration was in a mess. The production of mailing labels for 500 clients was farmed out. The labels were needed three times a week and were constantly being revised and updated but, because the work was done outside, the up-dates themselves were always out of date. Nora's husband was involved in computers in his work and suggested that the firm buy a micro and computerize the mailing list. This was early days, before packages were as well developed as they are now, and so he offered to write a mailing program for them.

A computer was duly purchased and arrived and sat on Nora's desk in a box. She left it there for a few days and then gingerly unpacked it. Nothing seemed to work. It was suggested that she look in the manual, but that was no use, partly owing to the usual incomprehensibility of that kind of manual, but in this case there was an extra difficulty: the computer was a special modified version of the Apple and the manual did not include the modifications. It soon became apparent that no progress would be made at work and so Nora took the computer home for her husband to write the program. This he did, but it took some time to perfect; the strain of her husband's involvement at a time when the marriage was breaking up became too much for Nora, and before the program was finally running smoothly – completely debugged – she took it back to the office. So she found herself in a situation where, although she had a good idea how the program worked, she also knew that it was not completely finished and foolproof. She was stranded with a task to perform on the computer, no one to ask for help and an office who expected her to succeed and who assumed that everything was fine.

Nora now found herself struggling to learn and operate new equipment. She had always been nervous of technical things – hi-fi equipment and so forth – and now she had to deal with a computer to which was attached a strong emotional charge because of the association with her husband. She had been a dutiful wife and mother for twenty years and now felt herself suddenly unwanted. She felt that she must either find new reserves, new methods of survival, or go under. She really had no choice, with three sons to continue to bring up, and, as she said, 'Something cleared in me at the crisis. I could not get any lower and the requirement to survive is so basic that it didn't seem to matter. When you have been through fire you emerge with great courage. I also began to get a feeling of my own value which had been dormant – or non-existent – before. I *had* to deal with the machine. There was no choice. That brought out the qualities of the fighting spirit, an inner strength at the point of desperation.' She had found a bootstrap with which to pull herself up and carry on.

This was the first time in her life, although she had a degree and was now in her forties, that she had taken something over completely and was faced with the need to develop her own skills unaided. She had to keep up the pretence that she knew what she was doing. She entered the 500 addresses successfully and did her first set of mailing labels. The outside system was kept on in parallel for a month but was then dropped as everything went smoothly. She had to learn much more than how to operate the labels system, since it is necessary to learn how to make backup copies and do other essential 'housekeeping' routines on a microcomputer. She also developed (an essential part of using a computer) safety-net routines. There was always the spectre of disaster in the possibility of a failure to get out the bulletins on which the company's business depended. She always kept two or three sets of labels ahead of requirement, which meant that in the last resort she had an up-to-date hard copy and could even, if necessary, type them out by hand. This never happened.

After some time, when the mailing labels' operation was going smoothly, she noticed that the computer was sitting unused for three days a week. She also observed that the firm's accounts were in a muddle. There were constant difficulties on the sales side, which operated on a card-index system and where many mistakes were made, causing ripples of trouble throughout the business. The accountant suggested using the computer. She began to wonder about book-keeping packages for the computer. Someone mentioned a 'chap across the corridor' who worked for a different firm but was using a computer for accounts and Nora talked to him. He was using an Apple, which was compatible with her machine, and told here where he had purchased his accounts package, said it was brilliant and that the salesman had been marvellously helpful.

Here was a package working, with a helpful supplier. Nora talked to the accountant, who gave her a list of questions to ask. As far as she was concerned it was just a list of words – she did not understand the meaning of any of them. She went along to the computer sales company and put the questions. She did not really understand the replies, but she noted down the crucial 'Yes' and 'No' and it all tallied with what the accountant required. The firm agreed to the purchase and the packages arrived, plus two hours' free tuition. Nora did not know what a balance was, but she had been told to enter the balances and get started. It was now January and the year began for that firm in August, so she went back to the books and entered every item from August to the end of December in order to achieve a balance. She did not at first understand about 'In' and 'Out' or how to enter a credit and terms like 'aged debtors' seemed like Sanskrit. However, she gradually learned about book keeping and also a lot about computers. By the end of the year she had learned how to operate a complicated financial package, had brought the sales ledger up to date and impressed the accountants.

The next disaster occurred when, after Nora had learned to operate the mailing-label system and the sales ledger, she taught the regular employees how to do the same. Although the initial skills are hard to acquire without guidance, they are fairly easy to pick up at a certain level with tuition, and Nora realized that she had worked herself out of a job and was no longer needed. She walked home from work one night and, desperate and on the verge of tears, called in at some friends for comfort. They advised her to look now for something that she could do on her own, saying that she was used to being her own boss, was quick to learn and worked better alone. If she set up as a consultant she could go into places where people would be pleased to see her and pleased to see the back of her. They suggested that, as an able woman, she would always be a threat to men and also to many other women, who would not like her because she was efficient.

This advice influenced her; she went home and reviewed her past life and decided that she must start something from scratch. She was fed up with translating and felt that she needed a new skill. The only thing that she felt at all encouraged about had been her relative and limited success with the computer. She thought that as she had been useful starting the accounts system for one firm, others would perhaps want her to do the same for them. She was prepared to do anything to gain independence and decided to buy her own computer. She got a quote for an Apple and a full set of accounts packages, Visicalc for financial forecasting, a word processor and a database. She bought the lot and, while still at the firm where she felt redundant, managed to acquire, with the help of relations and friends, two customers for whom she did the accounts for a total of £300 per month. This seemed enough to take the plunge, so she resigned and went freelance. After a year and a half she has reached the point where she will have to turn down more work.

That is Nora's story. How did she manage it? What factors worked for and against her? The aspects that stand out most strikingly are courage and persistence. But Nora feels that these were born of despair, and are not personal characteristics. She also had a certain amount of good fortune in that she was well educated and had friends and relations who could help and encourage her. Finance is always a problem. Other people can rarely solve one's income problems, but loans of capital to purchase equipment are a different matter and Nora was helped by her brother in this.

Even so, many people would feel that to take on computing without a science background, with no experience and in middle age is an achievement. Nora feels that there are many characteristics connected with being female which are a positive help in such a task, perhaps the most important of which is flexibility. Whether it is a female characteristic or the consequence of that stripping of self-respect and certainty about one's values and principles which comes from motherhood (the humiliating occasions when you hear yourself screaming at your children in precisely the way you vowed you never would), it is certainly true that most women have learned to be flexible, malleable, to wrap themselves around a situation as it is rather than as it ought to be.

Mastering a discipline as different from what we have been used to or educated for as computing is for most people over twenty-five something that involves not only great flexibility of mind but also a ready ability to appreciate individual facts and deduce new conclusions from imperfectly understood and insufficient or inadequately presented data. Nora found that, although she never bothered to master the internal intricacies of the computer, but only the programs it runs, when things went wrong she was nevertheless often quicker at finding a diagnostic clue than either her husband or the technicians who came to repair the equipment.

She was helped by technical people and thinks that she got especially good treatment for two reasons, both indirectly connected with being female. She had grasped fairly early on that even the experts are often completely at a loss when things go wrong and cannot always give a quick answer as to whether something is possible or not. This made her careful in her phrasing of requests and reasonable in her expectations about results. She thinks that they sensed this and were especially helpful as a result. She was also able to direct them in a way that was helpful. At an early stage when working for the first firm, a demonstration of electronic mail had been given. The demonstration included a program to draw Mickey Mouse on the screen – a totally irrelevant thing to do, which had no sensible link with the business of electronic mail, but was used as a sales gimmick. Nora was astonished that it was the only thing that seemed to interest the men and was the main topic of their conversation afterwards. Running wild after an abstraction (graphics), they had failed to exercise critical judgement on the matter in hand.

She often needed help and on such occasions nearly always had to turn to the suppliers of the computer or the software. She always got the help she needed, often involving the suppliers in services that went far beyond the call of duty. This is one of the problems with new technology: there are not enough sources of help, either in the form of courses or consultancy or literature, and thus a very heavy burden is placed on the shoulders of suppliers, who should not really have to teach as well as sell. Because there is no obligation, such help has to be sought delicately and tactfully, and cannot be insisted on as a right. Once again, a woman often finds it easier to ask for and receive such help and, therefore, for whatever reason, has a special advantage and fewer hang-ups at such moments.

Nora soon found that on the many occasions when the service men came out, most willingly and helpfully, to get the machine going or sort out some problem, they wasted hours following up some different and irrelevant matter which fascinated them but merely delayed the solution of the problem in hand. They loved the computer for itself, whereas she loved it only for what it could do. With tactful direction she could get better work out of them than they could have provided without her.

Not being fascinated by the computer as such, Nora also quickly appreciated the limitations and deficiencies of many systems. The inadequacies were usually in the software, and it was here that she learned to ask the searching questions that won her a reputation for being proof against wool over the eyes or slick sales talk. She feels that her clients also value her plain speaking. She describes quite openly the limits of what she and her computer system, hardware and programs, can do. This is still sufficiently unusual in a world that has developed a reputation for being dominated by 'cowboy' salesmen that she has on occasion been asked by astonished business men what on earth someone like her is doing in a field like this.

The main qualities that have enabled Nora to survive and, though not yet triumph, at least start on the road to success, seem to be three. The first is a sustained determination and dogged persistence; the second a concern for the practical, for the important and essential detail; the third an ability to communicate with people, to get help when and from whom she needed it, usually by unorthodox methods since no standard procedures existed. She also needed some help with capital and with references from friends. You have to have luck, but it is perseverance that enables you to take advantage of that luck when it crops up.

## Drusilla

Drusilla is the woman in this collection of examples who has relied most on, and worked most closely with, her husband. She read music and Anglo Saxon at Cambridge; did a secretarial course and got a job as a secretary but made such an appalling one that she quickly gave it up; went to Persia to record folk music and returned to work in a library. There she saw that people with qualifications which, though less than her own, were more specific earned much more money, so she decided to qualify as a librarian. She also did a week's introduction to book indexing and it was to this that she turned when she needed work at home after having children. She compiled between thirty and forty manual indexes before turning to a computer.

Drusilla's husband, Hilary, is a doctor working in cancer research. His brother has written a particularly sophisticated BASIC interpreter (XBASIC) while working in the mechanical engineering field at a university. Computers were not, therefore, unfamiliar to this family, and it seemed to them 'so obvious that indexing *should* be done on a computer.'

The typing in, editing and re-editing of entries, the frequent entry of the same long and difficult words or phrases, the cross-referencing of so many items, the sorting and paginating – these were all better done using a computer and the opportunities for clerical error much reduced. Paginating in particular can be a nightmare by hand, as it is often necessary to index a book without knowing the page numbers in the first instance, and then paginate only at the last minute when the publisher finalizes the numbering. Made-up numbers therefore have to be entered and later transformed into the real ones. This is the work of a few moments to a correctly programmed computer, but of many hours, stretching often to days, to a human operator.

Three years ago the Calverts decided to buy a computer for which Hilary would write an indexing program for Drusilla to use. The budget was tight with two small children and another expected and so they bought a kit (the Tuscan S100) fo £299 and built it themselves. It became apparent almost immediately that the 1K memory was not going to be sufficient to hold the program, let alone an index, so they spent another £300 on 64K of memory (RAM) to work with. Hilary built the machine and it worked well after a few initial hiccups. Then he wrote the program. This machine was a tape-based system and, although a vast improvement on a manual system, was nonetheless quite slow. Within eight months Drusilla had earned enough extra money to be able to add a disk drive and an operating system. Later they bought two more disk drives, a monitor (to use instead of a television screen) and a compiler, which makes the program run faster. Partly as a result of Drusilla's comments and partly to satisfy his own perfectionism, Hilary has re-written the program many times.

At some period during the first six months of operation Drusilla revealed to the Society of Indexers that she was using a computer. They reacted with great excitement, asked her to address a meeting and generally began treating her as their resident computer expert. Everyone in the Society is what she calls 'twitched and worried about computers, although they are not prepared to buy them or do anything positive about it'. Drusilla feels that their fears are well founded. She and Hilary were encouraged to start selling their program and several of the fifteen people who have bought it have been able to do a phenomenal amount of extra business. Many of them have also fed back comments and asked for extra features, such as bold and italic typefaces for page numbering in indexes to indicate illustrations or particular entries of that kind. One customer, very hesitant and difficult in the early stages, wrote to them the other day to congratulate them on an improved version which they had sent out, saying: 'What can I say? Excellence is added to excellence!'

Drusilla is confident that professional indexing, using a good program like hers which allies the brainpower and judgement of the indexer with the facilities of the computer, has an interesting future. Indexes are necessary not merely for books. The databases held on computer all around the world can be accessed and searched by individuals and organizations for a fee. However, payment is made only if the item searched for is actually found. Hence a good index, likely to result in a successful search, is vital to commercial success. The kinds of automatic indexing provided by a computer program which does not ally itself to professional skill are unlikely to have the cross-referencing and detail that will increasingly become necessary. Indexing will survive as a profession, but it looks as if it will need to become computerized in a professional way. It is a function that has always been carried out by a largely home-based group of people.

Drusilla has been involved not merely in learning to use a computer, but also in producing a professional and marketable piece of software. She has had more support and help to hand than any of the other examples – indeed her role has often been to restrain rather than push ahead. She did not just sit on the sidelines, however, and is an excellent example of how to turn the power of new technology to serve a cottage industry. She embarked on her new career while her children were still young, and, although she had never managed to find a job that really satisfied her in the days when she was young and highly qualified, now she has interesting work which she can take on as it suits her timetable and which she could expand into a fully fledged business later if she wished.

### Kate

Kate Jennings did not stay on at school or go to university, but took a secretarial course and followed the time-honoured route of starting as a secretary and working her way up. She came into computing with a set of skills that have proved to be unexpectedly useful and has taken word processing and related skills by the horns.

Once Kate's children were out of nappies, it became obvious that the family needed more money and also that she was rapidly becoming bored. She started to look around for work and to begin with did typing at home, which suited very well while the children were still very small, but for which her enthusiasm did not last long. The subject of indexing books was suggested as a more interesting alternative and she was advised that it would be much easier and more fun on a computer.

Kate borrowed a computer from her family and, although it seemed incomprehensible at first, succeeded in making a backup copy of the Wordstar word-processing package with which she was beginning.

Wordstar is extremely comprehensive and if you can master this program most other word-processing programs seem fairly simple in comparison. It covers almost everything that even the most difficult of customers might require: it has the ability to change page size and margins to any length; it has the power to move around a document very fast; tabulation is straightforward, including decimal tabs so that columns of figures are automatically lined up. All standard word-processing features are included, such as moving blocks of text around, search commands, etc. One of the best features is that it marks a line on the screen to show a page break (i.e. where a new page starts), and this, with complicated documents where layout is important, is a tremendous asset.

To begin with Kate did not realize (or understand the significance) that the computer she had borrowed was partly home-built and that various wires had been soldered in incorrectly. Each time she rang to say the machine had crashed she was gently rebuked and told it must be 'human error'. Fortunately, eventually this was found not to be the case! When at a later stage the computer continued to crash, she discovered that it did not have the necessary fan for keeping it cool and, therefore, whenever there were thunderstorms it became unhappy and crashed again; even the high spirits of children playing could upset it. However, these became minor problems in the light of the greater difficulties to come.

Very quickly Kate had to come to a decision – was she going to spend money or should she forget it all? By this time, however, she had caught the computing bug and was determined to pursue it. So her next step was to buy what seemed at the time to be a very expensive printer – £1000 with VAT. However, after two weeks of printing out at fifteen characters a second, which sounds a lot but in truth is very slow, Kate realized that she needed something better and began trying out various other printers. This was an unusual privilege, but had the almost disastrous consequence that every time she changed a piece of equipment, sometimes a small element in the total system, some vital alternation was forgotten – to change the switches inside the machine or to exchange a parallel for a serial cable, etc. – and the whole operation was brought to a halt, only to be started again by taking them back to base.

The publishers for whom Kate had embarked on typing a book in camera-ready form (i.e. to be printed direct from the copy she supplied) preferred Qume printers, and this was what she eventually bought. It was considerably more expensive than her original printer – over £2000 with VAT. Again, she had the problem of getting it to work with the computer and in fact she experienced considerable difficulty in getting a machine that functioned properly. Kate's experience in this respect was exceptionally bad, but the problems of getting the right printer with the right software and making the correct hardware and software connections are well known. To have as your first major project a book to be prepared in camera-ready form for the printers is also ambitious, to say the least, though it is probably only through tackling difficult jobs that the major skills are acquired.

For the book on which Kate was working to be produced camera-ready meant that she was involved at every stage from the first draft to the final print out. There were a set number of lines to the page with the headings and page numbers alternating their position for odd and even pages and the publishers' house style and copy editing had to be incorporated, as well as complicated tables and, finally, the index, both camera ready and using an indexing program to do most of the indexing work. The publishers also preferred to have proportional spacing if possible and it was particularly for this that she had bought the more expensive Qume. However, she had not realized that, although the printer may be capable of it, if the word-processing software is not, the word-processing software is the stronger of the two and so takes no notice of the printer. With the help of a student working temporarily in computing, she eventually discovered that Wordstar could be patched to do proportional spacing by reducing the space between the smaller letters – e.g. the 'i' and the '1' – and varying the space size for the other letters, which also meant that she could use standard daisy wheels rather than the special proportionally spaced ones. It then became a question of using it constantly to see where the letters did not look right and Kate had to learn a little about machine code in order to be able to do it herself. Eventually she achieved the proportional spacing she was looking for.

Meanwhile, she had bought a sheet feeder for the Qume (to feed single sheets of paper into the printer continuously) so that the final print out of the camera-ready book could be done easily and accurately. Two weeks before she was due to do the final print out, the sheet feeder broke and had to go back to the manufacturers. Then on the day she actually started the print out, everything went wrong. Gobbledygook was printed out. She had only three days in which to produce the final copy, but fortunately a friend who knew something about computers suggested that they look at the plugs on the cable between the computer and the printer. There lay the problem and they were quickly soldered back together again in time for Kate to complete her job.

During the first year of learning word processing Kate was asked by a variety of people to produce unusually complicated layouts for documents. As a result she got to know Wordstar inside out and decided that she should set herself up to train other people. She started by making copious notes so that she could use them as a guide for herself when training. However, after a great deal of work on them she felt that she should sell them alongside the training she offered, and this she now does almost every time she trains anybody new. Having had no intelligible documentation when she started herself, she has taken trouble to make sure that her own notes cover all the tricks and difficulties involved in Wordstar and, sold at £10 each, they now make a steady addition to her income. She has also found, however, that the training usually has to go beyond just word processing and include some knowledge of the computer as well – how to take copies, to find out the amount of space on a disk, etc.

Kate embarked on training word processing exactly a year after she had taken her own first steps in computing and throughout that time she had consistently had more work than she could handle and already had someone to help, so she decided it was time to buy her own computer. It was also clear that, with the volume of work she had, she needed a fast dot matrix printer for drafts, so she bought an Epson FX80 (the Qume does fifty-five characters per second and the Epson 160). She also bought an Epson portable computer to work on at the same time as the main computer.

Her next step was to learn a new word-processing program that had not long been on the market – Perfect Writer. She had the usual problems of not being able to make it work with her printer, but by now had enough experience not to have to take everything back to base. This software is in four parts which cover most office requirements: Perfect Writer, Perfect Speller, Perfect Filer, the database and Perfect Calc, the financial spreadsheet. They can either be bought separately or as an integrated package, meaning that a lot of the commands are the same throughout the different programs. Kate inevitably found herself learning the other programs as well as the word processor. As she had given up maths at the age of twelve and had not even taken O-level, the spreadsheet was the greatest challenge. Although she says she still does not really understand the more complicated aspects of it, she now uses it easily and can help other people understand how to use it. The database she found slightly more difficult. However, because the mailing list side of Wordstar is the least good from the keying-in point of view, she had already learned the early stages of dBase II (a complex database package) and has been using this for several months quite competently combined with MailMerge, the mailing facility that goes with Wordstar. Perfect Filer is a program that is very easy to use once you have set up the database, but that in itself is no mean feat. Before long, Kate was approached, as being one of the few people who knew it quite well, to put a large mailing list on it, to sort by county, by the record number and, finally, in alphabetcial order. This all had to be done in two weeks, but fortunately by working day and night in amongst their other work, she and her associates managed to do it.

Once Kate became experienced in training, it was suggested that she should do some word-processing demonstrations for a firm which sells computers. This inevitably required more learning, and once again she found the first one or two demonstrations were absolutely terrifying. In the last few months she has learned Perfect software, Peachtree software (which includes word processing, database and financial spreadsheet); a bit about Spellbinder (word processing), Supercalc (a well-known spreadsheet) and Indexer (the indexing program she used for the camera-ready book). Many people come to a demonstration uncertain of what they want and why they want it, but with a conviction that they *do* want it. It was necessary for Kate to learn all the above (and more) so that, coupled with the experience in office administration that she had gained before having children, she could give clear advice as to what would suit the buyer most.

Just two years after starting, Kate now has two computers, two printers, a sheet feeder for the letter-quality printer, every intention of shortly buying a third computer, and two part-time assistants to help with all the work. Also, for the first time since her children were born, the family has a live-in help, which became essential once she was working two regular days a week as well as doing the training and all the work at home. How has she done it? For several years before having children she worked as a secretary in varied jobs, gradually moving up the ladder but, nonetheless, still being not much more than a high-powered secretary/PA and this experience has been invaluable. It has meant that she has been able to put the computer to work in a particular way, to do better jobs that she already knew how to do by hand. Her parents helped to finance her in this. To set off from nowhere into computers is not easy and she feels that she could not have decided to make the financial commitment without their help.

Certainly Kate regrets nothing and has an immense feeling of achievement and sense of purpose which she did not have before. She also feels immense satisfaction from knowing that she is capable of holding her own in this high-technology world. She feels that more women might be willing to take the plunge if they were not frightened off by the very word 'computers': if they could be given a less daunting name, the response to them might be very different.

*Chapter 8*

# Rose, Sarah and Mary

Rose Deakin, Sarah Todd and Mary Palmer have all managed to acquire enough skills in computing to earn their living as professionals within the industry.

### Rose
I tell my own story because it is so closely linked to the theme of the book and because I think, of all the examples, I have probably entered the furthest into the computer world – not just using computers, but becoming part of the computer industry itself. Like the others, I had to have a sparking point. Once it has become clear that computing is a sensible trade for a woman then no particular incentive is needed; before this moment of general recognition there has to be an identifiable reason for taking such a step.

Mine was rage. I suffered a setback in career terms which was not unlike Nora's marriage (see Chapter 7), though less shattering because, for many women at least, work is less central to their lives and emotions than marriage.

The background to this rage was that I had been employed to transfer onto a mainframe computer data collected for a survey, and then analyse it using standard packages. Theoretically, a knowledge of computing is not required for such a task, though in practice it is very difficult with none.

Various wrangles took place; I felt that I could not continue to work in such circumstances, and decided to resign. After looking around for a while at rather unappetizing jobs in social research – a field which is heavily over-subscribed and in which I was unlikely to find a job easily – I decided that the aspect of the research in which I had recently been involved that had amused me most – despite its trauma – was computing. My first thoughts were about entering traditional mainframe computing. I had recently heard about microcomputers when enquiring among the computer people about ways of helping my fourteen-year-old son, who was frustrated at the lack of computing opportunity at school. Someone suggested that I go into micro rather than traditional computing, since it would solve so many of my problems. It was a new field and therefore one would not be expected to have twenty years' experience; I could buy a micro and work at home, thus solving the part-time problem; by teaching myself at home I would also solve the training problem, as there were in those days no training courses at all for microcomputing. It was the only idea that had given my spirits a lift in the last few months. It felt right and I decided to take the plunge.

It seemed as if the cost of a good starting machine might be in the middle hundreds and I could borrow that amount within the family, so I took the decision. I ended up spending over £1000 in the first place and considerably more over the ensuing year, but it has all been money well spent.

I spent a year struggling to master the intricacies of the computer – basic principles, the operating system, a programming language (Pascal) and even dabbling with machine code. I had not heard of hex or octal until those days, and, in spite of trying to improve my mind with an Open University maths course a few years previously, my comprehension of everything mathematical has always been very shaky. I worked and worked and often wondered whether anything would ever come of it. Luckily I enjoyed it, and I find the same fascination with the way it works that is observable in men. I also have a firmly held view that you reap what you sow, that hard work may go unrewarded for a time but the pay-off arrives in the end, and that, though you do not always take out of a system exactly the same as you put in, or at the same time or place, you usually get something equivalent. In this instance at least the philosophy proved correct. I can apply myself to things only if there is some tangible end in view and so, in order to learn to program, I had to find applications that needed programming and I ruthlessly canvassed my friends for jobs that they could think of, aspects of their current work that I could attempt to write programs to computerize. I would not charge, since I did not know what I could achieve in the first instance. My friends responded, as always, with sympathy and help, and I got a lot of stimulating work to do, in one case even paid work. A friend's child's fiancée had just graduated in computer studies using only mainframes and wanted some micro experience before starting work at CAP (one of the best-known firms of computer programmers and consultants). I paid him a contribution to his living expenses to come and work with me for a month and learned about programming techniques. After about six months of this I had mastered most of the basic skills and built a confidence and familiarity with the machine which was sufficient foundation for proceeding to something more ambitious.

My experiences on the large computer on which time had been booked at my last job had taught me that almost no one who uses a computer can do so successfully without advice and help from computer professionals. A computer professional, by definition, does not put a computer to the use for which it is designed. If he did he would not be a computer professional but a banker, or a statistician, or a flight controller, or an operations and research manager, or one of the other professional people whose work is made easier by computing tools. On large expensive machines a team of advisors is employed to help such people. Micros for business and professional use cost between £1000 – £5000; no one can afford a team of professionals to service them. On the other hand, they are if anything harder to use than large computers because the user has to learn to put data and instructions in and out and work the operating system as well as write programs or run packages. This is done for you on a big machine by a large army of intermediaries. So my idea was to learn about micros and then offer myself as a peripatetic advisory service to desperate businessmen.

It was a good idea and I think I could have worked it, but during the year that I had given myself to master computing many things happened to divert me. I purchased my equipment from the firm I now work for, Transam Microsystems. They had been one of the first British manufacturers to set up in business. The firm was started by its present directors, who came in not as computer professionals with a research and design team, but from the field of components' sales. They thought in terms of a shop, or, as we now call it, a showroom, and it was this aspect which I found comforting. Apart from the Byte shops, which had just started in 1979, I did not know of anywhere else where you could go and buy a microcomputer from a shop, rather than from a production centre or a mail-order firm. I knew that shops were open at certain hours, that one could go to them and ask for services, repairs if necessary, and perhaps, *in extremis,* help. In any case, they were there, identifiable and visible. The people seemed friendly and approachable.

During the first year I had constant problems and constant recourse to Transam for help with all kinds of things, including programming and matters far removed from their obligation to me as a customer. I had occasion to criticize the manuals that they produced and also to explain what I was trying to do. They perceived that my concern for the customer and the new computer public, which would consist of more than hobbyists and buffs, was a useful way of approaching sales and marketing. They needed someone to organize a software list for the computer that they manufactured and marketed, and precisely a year after I had first walked into their shop, they offered me a job.

I had to work extremely hard in order to keep on top of the job, especially feeling, as I did, rather underqualified to say the least. However, such is the general level of ignorance about computers in the world that a year later I found myself standing up in front of an audience composed of 200 senior civil servants – 95 per cent of whom were male – and lecturing them on the subject of database management. A few months previously I could not have defined the term myself and this, plus the exhilaration of succeeding in a man's world, made me laugh inwardly with glee and with the feeling of 'if they only knew.' The speaker before me had blinded them with science and spoken almost entirely in strings of initials on the subject of networking, so I did not have much difficulty in appearing in a favourable light. I later expanded the speech into a book which was published in 1983. I say this not simply to boast, but to try to give an idea of the comparative ease – comparative to any other technical profession – with which one can still break into computing. It is early days and the shortage of manpower, and particularly womanpower, articulation and literacy is chronic: another reason, surely, for seizing the opportunity and not sitting about waiting until it is an oversubscribed profession like all the rest.

As with Nora in the previous chapter, one of the questions – in answer to the 'Yes it is all right for you but I just haven't got those qualities' kind of response – is: how was this achieved? I had the same non-science background, which was actually worse than Nora's, as languages are now regarded as quite a reasonable preparation for computing, whereas no one would say that about history as it was then taught. I had a crisis which made me review my life and make decisions. I wanted to find work consistent with the later stages of mothering. I had already brushed with computers and found myself attracted to them. Once I had taken the decision, I had no choice. For other, but not dissimilar, reasons I had to make a go of it and so courage and determination were provided – an inner resource, a bootstrap, was found.

It is important perhaps to stress that I was not, am not and never shall be good at maths. Most people assume that I am because I can manage a computer, but I have a distinct weakness in that area. When I signed on for an Open University maths foundation course I had last touched maths at O-level (GCE in those days) twenty years before and could not even remember how to do long division. But, funnily enough, it is computing that has made me understand the concept of xy coordinates, Cartesian axes or what you will, not all the theoretically based maths courses in the world. Computing is actually much easier than maths since the difficulty is not absolute or conceptual but more to do with the unaccustomed and novel approach to problems – novel at least to those of us who suffered an education that allowed us to give up all sciences at the age of twelve.

The actual practicalities of getting started were: I was given the money by my parents and I bought a computer, and a year later a printer. I bought a book on programming in Pascal, entitled *A Practical Introduction to Pascal* by Wilson and Addyman,* and a couple of books on Z80 machine code

*revised edition, Macmillan, 1982

programming, and I sat with my computer until I could do it. I had to have help, without which I might have foundered completely, but, equally, there is always a limit to the amount of help people have time to give you. You really have to do most of it yourself. These days, although help is still pretty vital, there are training courses and more books that can be used as aids so that people without friends in the trade should be able to manage. A friendly and helpful supplier will always be a vital prerequisite.

I have found the same kind of female characteristics useful as have been mentioned by the other women in these chapters. First, I have a more results-oriented (to use computer speak) approach than is common with most men and this has been invaluable. During the nightmare period of my previous job, we had had discussions with a French agency with whom we were collaborating on a piece of research. The research was founded on premises which, though probably valid, had certainly never been questioned or tested. The core of it depended on a massive questionnaire, difficult and expensive to administer. The French delegate, female, was generally regarded as a pest because she would interrupt the proceedings from time to time to say *'Mais qu'est ce que le but de cette questionnaire?'* ('What is the *purpose* of this questionnaire?') No one ever answered her, but I thought it came under the heading of 'Good Question'. It is also a question which, with an appropriate target, needs asking regularly in computing and I am able to ask it with the interests of the end user (customer, person who actually operates and uses the micro) in mind.

I have also, like Nora, found help relatively easy to get. I knew from the start that I would need it and spent a lot of time trying to make myself acceptable so that I would be able to get it. I emphatically do not mean to imply here the use of sex or flirtation or sexual manipulation. Rather I mean the ways in which women have learned to communicate; to ask for help without being aggressive; to indicate failings without implied criticism (because as Nora found, one recognizes the difficulties, and sees, as with a child learning to walk, talk or control itself, the immensity of the task); to indicate the nature of the assistance required and so short-cut the running wild after abstractions. I have, more than her, felt that I sometimes had extra assistance because women were unusual in this field and men appreciated and were entertained by the novelty.

Now that I work as a sales consultant, I still feel that there are some ways in which I have something special to offer by being female. I think that I have been able to advise and assist the male customers particularly well because they do not feel threatened by me, because I have learned to communicate and because I am concerned with the practicalities of their needs rather than the beauty of any particular machine. As one person said, I am 'into customer solutions.' This may not be the preserve of women, but it is their very special contribution and one which the whole industry needs. This is one reason why it is as important for men as it is for women that women become more involved in computers and computing.

## Sarah

Sarah Todd had always been treated like a boy at home, building machines and playing with bricks rather than dolls when she was little. When it came to choosing whether to go for arts or sciences for her A-level speciality she chose science because she 'wanted to beat all the boys. I knew that I could do better than them at science.' She always made sure at school that, whatever else, she did better than the boys.

She read chemistry at Oxford and only quite enjoyed it. She began to be somewhat disillusioned with the subject and this disillusionment was increased by her experience working in the vacations at British Petroleum where, she found, there was 'a complete lack of things to be done' and everyone was sitting around doing very little. All the chemistry jobs that she looked at when thinking about her future seemed un-exciting and 'BP-ish'. By this she meant large company and un-urgent in aspect.

In her vacation jobs at BP she had had the opportunity to play around on the computers and was attracted to the subject, perhaps because she had always been fascinated by maths. When it came to looking for a job she searched particularly for those that, while requiring a degree, did not specify a particular subject. These mostly seemed to be in computing, and especially programming, where people were often trained on the job. She was also quite interested in the idea of selling as such.

In November 1983 she started work as 'trainee sales engineer' for a new microcomputer to be launched in January 1984 and called the Wren Executive. This is a computer which has the computing part and the vital peripherals – screen and disk drives – packed into a single container. It has some new design concepts and a lot of 'bundled' (free) software. As Sarah had to acquaint herself with the technicalities of computing in a very short time it is difficult to describe her experience without reference to technical terms. These are all explained in Chapter 11 and your bewilderment on reading these words may be matched only by hers in the first few days of her new job. In a short space of time she had to learn about the basic concepts of microcomputing, an operating system (CP/M2.2) and its upgrade (CP/M+, with comparisons), BBC BASIC and graphics, a whole range of office software including time management, word processor, database and spread-sheet, and communications to Prestel and Micronet 800. She also had to be sufficiently familiar with the hardware and design of the machine to be able to answer first-line technical questions. The grapevine reported that the boys at BP had shaken their heads when they heard that she had got this job. When asked why, the answer was, 'She doesn't know anything about computers'. Sarah laughed at this and said, 'Ah, but what *they* don't know is that I spent all my time at BP when there was nothing to do playing around with the computer.'

She had plunged into the microcomputer world and acquired a challenging job which involved rapid learning of many new concepts and new techniques. She says that she found it quite baffling at first. She objected particularly to the CP/M operating system – it seemed silly to her – and she felt that she wanted to get on with learning the programs. Terms like 'booting up', needing a 'system' on a disk, the whole idea of an operating program just did not click for her. Then one day she realized what it was all about and that the operating system was the nerve-centre of the whole operation. Then 'suddenly it started to take off.'

The concepts behind the word-processor and spreadsheet programs that were bundled (provided free) with the Wren seemed quite easy to Sarah, though the actual commands took a little learning. She was not so happy with the database program at first, mostly because she had never heard of a database and did not know how it could be useful. She now thinks it is 'incredibly useful'. The Wren has fairly elaborate graphics, providing the user with the capability to draw pictures and graphs. Sarah said that she found these one of the hardest features to learn to use because she did not see them as very important in the everyday use of the machine, though it is an aspect which interests customers when they have demonstrations of the computer.

Sarah has helped at two major computer exhibitions – Compec and the *Which Computer?* show – and has demonstrated the Wren to innumerable customers and even taken part in the training of other sales people. She still has a little trouble remembering all the hardware details and says that she still does not know how the machine works and what goes on inside – all the binary part and how the chips and circuitry work. She cannot learn anything until she understands how it works and has to take in the conceptual part first; the details come second. She plans to tackle that soon, when she has time.

The main satisfaction has been 'grasping something new'. She enjoys demonstrating and selling as well, and even here it is necessary to continue learning, though in a different way, to improve skills as well as knowledge. She is not particularly conscious of being a woman in a man's world and feels that she is treated as an equal by her colleagues. At BP she thinks that she was one of two women chemists in her building and she felt she was a curiosity. 'BP is like Oxford – it has only just gone co-ed.' It seemed as if all the women there were young and 'they do not move up as fast as the men.' At all the interviews that she attended for traditional jobs she was asked whether she had any plans for getting married. She found this odd, since it is not marriage but motherhood that causes women to stop working. She hopes that the micro world will be less hidebound.

Sarah's example is interesting because she is young and just embarking on her career, rather than re-entering like most of the other examples I have used, or changing tack. She took a chemistry degree, but this involved no computing at all. She picked up what she could about computers when working on vacation jobs, but came almost entirely green to the field of microcomputing to take on an interesting job with in-service training and considerable responsibility attached to it. At the time of writing, she has been doing it for only four months, but is enjoying it and is reasonably successful at it.

### Mary

Mary Palmer is the only woman in this group to have had some formal training in computing. After an interesting and successful decade during which she had written two books, taught in a university and done a number of other jobs, she felt attracted to the idea of going into business. At first she speculated on the idea of starting her own business, but her attention was caught one day by an advertisement for a Manpower Services Commission training course providing training in skills such as computing and systems analysis.

This was the TOPS Business Experience course. Mary had not had much business experience but her interest in the subject had been enough to persuade the selection group to take her on. In this she was lucky because the catch-22 for women is that you can only go on such a course if you have business experience and the majority of women under forty (the technical age limit) are unlikely as yet to have had much opportunity. There were three women among the sixteen members of the course and Mary thinks that that was about average.

The syllabus included subject matter necessary to pass the examination which led to a certificate from the National Computing Centre. It also contained as much as possible of the more modern teaching on the subject of systems analysis. Teaching was given in the BASIC and COBOL programming languages, and students carried out a case study involving the simulation of a proper exercise in systems analysis on a real business situation. Some students grumbled about the NCC syllabus because it is updated fairly infrequently and, they felt, did not keep up with changing ideas in the computing world. Some of the teaching was also rather low level, but by and large the course did what it set out to do; equip people with skills that would help them to find jobs. In order to qualify for money from the MSC, the firm that provided the course had to show that a good proportion of its students were finding work. It claimed to do this partly by selecting students carefully and, for those courses that involved practical placements, maintaining a good reputation with employers for matching their needs.

While on the course, the students were paid £25 per week and the training organization was also paid a fee per student. Mary found the work both exciting and difficult. There were sixteen Televideo terminals to work at, and one man to service them. This he did, but with only intermittent success. Terminals frequently collapsed and died, which provided a valuable illustration of the frailty and fallibility of computers. The main difficulty for Mary was the absolute necessity of disciplined thinking. In the kind of research and teaching work in which she had previously been involved, work which essentially demanded exploration and experimentation with ideas, she had been accustomed to allowing her mind to float freely, following up new ideas and associations. Computing needed other methods and had no connection with what she knew already. She felt a fear of humiliation at the keyboard. Though she was accustomed to a keyboard from her writing activities, she sometimes felt quite mad, sitting at a computer terminal trying to compile a COBOL program and watching idiot mistakes come up. There seemed to be something irrevocable about entering an instruction on to the computer, or corrupting data which she urgently required. It was very daunting, and probably worse because she had no experience of home computers. She thought that those who had a Sinclair Spectrum or the equivalent at home managed better, though the subject matter was different.

Mary's intellectual grasp of what the computer could do developed much faster than her personal ability to make it do what she wanted. She was frustrated at seeing how to tackle subjects but actually not being able. She could see the uses of computers in business and was excited by the whole exercise. She has 'learned to appreciate and have a respect for syntax.' She can see that the machine needs a framework within which to operate even if it is not plain English and requires to be translated effectively. The course lasted only sixteen weeks, so that the feeling of inadequacy was a temporary aspect of tackling a new skill at a stage in life when one expects to feel competent and in control. Computers are great levellers and the triumph towards the end of such a course, when achievements begin to accumulate, is compensation for the anguish in the early stages.

The course finished in November 1983. Mary was advised that she would probably find it hard to get a job as a systems analyst because, at thirty-three, she was too old. Firms prefer to take on youngsters, train them and pay them correspondingly less. The advice was to look in the *Computer User's Yearbook* for firms with large data-processing departments and write around to them. She did so and was offered four jobs – from two large commercial firms, a software house and a public-sector organization. She chose one of the large commercial firms and began work in January 1984.

Mary has a good network of influential friends and an interesting past history. Nonetheless, she had on two previous occasions failed to find an opening that suited her in the business world and at the time of her application for the TOPS course she was technically unemployed. With a computer qualification the position seemed quite different. It gave firms some reason for looking at her application and noticing her abilities in other areas, such as writing, public speaking and administration. It enabled her to understand the newspapers and the jargon where previously, when scanning papers for jobs in computing, she had not been able to understand more than half the words used in the advertisements. Now 'I deal every day with real live programmers and analysts and do not feel one-hundred-per-cent foolish even though I do not understand ninety per cent of what they say. The ten per cent that I do understand is a foothold that gets bigger and bigger.'

*Chapter 9*

# Christine and Marjorie

Christine Bloomfield and Marjorie Stewart are examples of women using computers at home for self-improvement or pleasure. They are neither of them, at the moment, earning money with their computers, but may do so later.

### Christine

Christine Bloomfield left school at sixteen and went to work in a bank which dealt with bullion and foreign exchange. She enjoyed the work, which involved using VDUs (visual display units, or computer terminals). The girls were moved around to different floors with different machines and jobs to learn at regular intervals, so it did not become boring as VDU work usually does. She worked there until she had her little boy, five years ago when she was twenty-seven.

While she was at home looking after her son she decided that she 'did not want to look silly' when she went back to work and that she would also like to learn what went on behind the VDU – 'to find out how they really worked rather than just pressing a key'. She went along to her local library and asked whether there were any courses on computing. She was given the literature of the Haringey Women's Technical Training Centre (WTEC) which offered among other things an evening course in 'Computer Basics'.

This describes itself as a course 'aimed at increasing women's confidence in using computers. Geared to meet the needs of women interested in finding out about computers, wishing to try a new skill, or women whose jobs are likely to be affected by new technology. The course assumes no previous knowledge. To register, turn up on the night.' Since all the TOPS courses have the requirement that those attending be unemployed, this is a course that caters for a wide range of people. The same centre offered courses in electronics, home maintenance (domestic water systems, lighting, woodwork, repair, maintenance and emergencies) and a range of practical subjects. Full-time courses were also available with a creche for children provided.

There were about fifteen women on the course, some housewives like Christine who 'wanted to find out more', some unemployed and some women working in offices which were planning to introduce computers and who, like Christine, did not wish to be caught looking silly when the time came. Christine did the course and was then encouraged by the tutors to do another one: Programming in BASIC. This taught the first steps in programming in an efficient and systematic way, using analogies such as knitting and other traditionally female occupations. Christine said that the course members were encouraged to think along the same lines. In programming a standard letter they were told to think first of what might be necessary. For knitting you need wool, needles and a pattern; for programming a letter you need to have a way of entering the name and then the address into the standard pattern of the letter. This description may not do the teaching justice, but it is an interesting example of an attempt to teach women in a special way and avoid the usual car analogy.

When she had successfully finished the programming course Christine turned her mind to word processing. The tutors at the women's centre also taught at the Middlesex Polytechnic and, as a result, she went on a word-processing course there. The course was advertised in the local paper and she might have found it in that way, but in fact it was the personal contact that took her there. It seems that it is only necessary to make an initial effort; after the first move you are swept along by the tide of other people's enthusiasm – at least if you are as worth teaching as Christine clearly is. The previous courses had been evening courses, but this one took place in the daytime. Again, Christine's justification was that she 'wanted to keep her ideas up and know what they were talking about when she went back to work.'

Now, having passed through computer basics, elementary programming and a word-processing course, Christine is tackling book keeping. This is not a computer course, but a course in manual book keeping. It seems very likely that she will find herself in a situation where a knowledge of computing and a knowledge of book keeping will come together to provide a very useful asset both to her and to some future employer. She has bought herself a Commodore 64 with disk drives and, although she says that she does it only to keep up, it seems more likely that she will get well ahead when she returns to work. She is a prime example of someone who is using the years of child-rearing to pursue some further skill and, while attending courses which she says 'give women a better view to life, and an interest', equipping herself for the future in a way that is much more open to women than to most men with their unbroken careers.

*Note.* Soon after the above was written, Christine was offered a job working for a microcomputer systems house. Her knowledge of computing combined with office skills seemed invaluable in such circumstances.

### Marjorie

Marjorie Stewart has always been interested in genealogy. She is a teacher and proposed after retirement to take up semi-professionally what had previously been just a hobby. She first thought about getting a computer because there were so many notes to be collected when studying public records, parish registers and inscriptions on gravestones – grist to the mill of genealogists.

It is possible that the idea would never have got off the ground if she had not happened to meet someone with a computer and see for herself just what was involved. She had previously looked at magazines and found them full of words she did not understand, but when she saw the computer being used to write a book with a word-processing package she realized that 'given the right program, you're off' without needing to know about programming. Programming was definitely not for her, as her mind did not work that way and she found it too time consuming. She tried out the computer and found that it was 'just a typewriter'. This gave her the confidence to proceed.

She decided to start with a Sinclair ZX81 in order to gain some familiarity with the computer. It was not right for her, however, as she wanted applications programs, not to learn about programming: she wanted to learn to drive, not to be a motor mechanic. Luckily for her, the boy across the road was longing to become involved with computers and he dropped in regularly to sort her out. He eventually bought it from her and she decided to buy an Apple instead.

She looked up a list of Apple dealers, went to the one that was geographically nearest and bought a new Apple computer. The shop was a general games shop, not a computer specialist, and though the people were very nice and helpful the service was not satisfactory. It is worth trying to discover why in order to give advice to future purchasers. Marjorie feels that it is probably important to go to a specialist shop, not a dealer in general electronic equipment or, as in her case, many non-electronic things as well. She has recently purchased a Tandy portable computer for use when taking notes in libraries, and this she purchased from a large Tandy shop in Edinburgh. She feels that she has had excellent service from there, although in London, where the shops that she has used for Tandy equipment were smaller and more general purpose, the service has been much less good. Service in computing does not mean being polite and helpful behind the counter; most people are probably that, and all are well intentioned. It means knowing how to sort out problems and generally deliver the goods to the customer over a wide range of computing specialities.

Where Marjorie's original supplier failed was in his promise to write a program for her that would handle her genealogical material; basically, a data-handling program that could sort items into order and find them for her in response to her typing in a search word, typically a name. He never managed to deliver a program that worked, and probably wasted time and money on it himself. The Edinburgh Tandy shop, on the other hand, managed to track down for her a ready-made program that does just what she wants.

Currently, Marjorie is having a program written specially for her and she is confident that this will succeed. She has been able to specify much more clearly what she wants this time because she has attended meetings organized by the Society of Genealogists for people using computers. These meetings provide for an exchange of ideas and programs and help. The Society is anxious to catch people early and get a system going which everyone will follow, thus making the work of individual members far more useful. She finds that people are talking about the things that she wants to know about, such as how to lay out fields in the right way. Some of the members have written and published their own programs but, unfortunately from her point of view, they all seem to be going for the BBC and not Apples. The other thing she has found useful is their way of looking at things. As a teacher and not an office worker she has not been accustomed to thinking in terms of indexing, filing and recording information and she is picking up these methods of thought from her colleagues in the Society.

Once again, the interesting questions are: what were Marjorie's difficulties and how did she overcome them?

Marjorie says that the Apple came with four books, none of which she could really follow. When something did not work she did not know where to find the answer and often Roy, her willing helper, was also flummoxed. When they could not find how to get the machine to print, they tried looking up the word PRINT in each of the books, but found that it meant something quite different in computing and did not provide the answer The *Disk Operating System Manual* turned out to be the most useful, rather to her surprise. The surprise was partly based on the fact that the manual was entitled *DOS Manual* and she did not discover for a long time what that meant. The *Apple Tutorial* tried to teach her to program, but that she did not want to do. She tried to learn the words by studying the magazines and trying to make out how they were being used but, although this helped a little, it did not do enough. She says, 'It strikes me as all being a bit of a club.'

I asked Marjorie what she did and felt when she got completely stuck, and she smiled and said, 'I sent for Roy.' It seems to me to be a wonderful thing to have contact with a boy like this who is potty about computing and cannot afford a computer of the sophistication of Marjorie's. Everyone gains: he from the chance to get his hands on such a dream, you from the free and willing help of someone much better equipped to solve the problem than you are.

Marjorie is completely undismayed by her slow start with the computer. She clearly still feels interested in it and even gives the impression of being quite fond of it. She is determined to overcome the problems 'because given the right programs I shall be away.' There is such a lot that she wants to do, and not necessarily in order to make money, although she may make some.    She has had such benefit from the indexes to parish registers that other people have prepared that she is keen to make her contribution now that she has time, which so many people have not.... Indexing registers is one thing she means to do, and possibly also indexing the tombstone inscriptions in disappearing graveyards.

The Tandy portable computer has been easier to use than the Apple – mostly, she thinks, because it is in every way simpler; it cannot do so much, but what it does is easier to learn. The book is quite straightforward for the most part and, although she found the editing instructions confusing, this did not worry her as she did not need to edit her notes.

I asked, finally, about finance. Marjorie said that the equipment had been expensive and she usually avoids mentioning how much. However, people are not shocked if you buy yourself a car, and that costs much more. She was about to retire and saw the computer as 'my retirement present to myself.'

*Chapter 10*

# Points Arising
# from the Examples

The examples of women who have mastered some aspect of computing, usually microcomputing, illustrate in each case some individual attributes, but also show many common factors. In nearly every case there is evidence of unusual application and determination. This is perhaps inevitable at the moment when in Britain it is still a rather unusual course to take, but as the use of computers becomes more widespread it will cease to be so. However, it is at this time that the individuals who decide to try their hands can achieve the most startling results.

The situation is more advanced in the United States, where articles appear with subtitles such as: 'The winds of change are at hurricane force as more and more women venture into the previously male-dominated realm of the professional computer user'.[11] Examples are then given of women using computers in order to advance their studies at university; in publishing, especially in the burgeoning software departments; by joining the sales staff of computer stores; in public relations; accounting; law, where one woman said that she saw personal computers 'as a way for women to get a competitive edge in business. When I bought it, my practice was new and I was trying to break into an established community'. The article concludes that women's attitudes to computing are different from men's and much more serious, less linked to the idea of computers as toys or hobby material. 'They consider an understanding of computers as a way to get ahead in male-dominated professions'.

It seems that determination is necessary, together with a major effort and a somewhat serious approach to the subject. This sounds rather deadly, but it is true to say that in most of the cases illustrated here there was a certain amount of pleasure to be had as well. Although women have not the time in life (with their dual or triple roles) to take on this kind of thing purely for pleasure, the stimulation of a new and difficult task, the thrill felt at the various stages of achievement – conquering the slopes on the way to the peak – all these are not inconsiderable rewards to add to the personal advancement that is attached to the new skill.

If no very special personal qualities are necessary, most people nonetheless assume that you have to be clever to understand computers. The answer is that to understand computers you have to have a modicum of intelligence and a little previous education if you are not to have a terrible struggle. However, to quote Mary Shelley once more, 'A mind of moderate capacity, which closely pursues one study, must infallibly arrive at a great proficiency in that study.'* It is important to emphasise, too, that we are talking in the majority of cases not about understanding computers but about using them. The more you understand them the less trouble you will have in using them and everyone needs to know just a little, although the majority of computer-users do not need to know exactly how they work. The parallel with a car is not an exact one, because it is useful to understand more of the logic of the subject than is perhaps necessary with cars, but it will do. Everyone drives a car and only a small percentage of the population knows how to build or mend one. We think that we know less about the logic of cars than we probably do because they are so familiar and the basic logic feels like something that we have been born with. For future generations this will also apply to computers.

It is also necessary to remember that there are several levels at which one can operate in computing. Nora (Chapter 7), for instance, had considerable travail in mastering the computer from first principles of operating and had to learn not only how to use it but also how to do book keeping. This is a natural corollary of the fact that the computer does nothing useful on its own: it has to be applied to a professional skill or a problem. Once she had done this she was able to teach the other workers at her office to make use of the computer in a simple way following strict guidelines. The people concerned may not have been as intelligent as she was, and were certainly less well educated, but they had no difficulty in learning to use the computer at a level that was simpler and required less skill and innovation. In this kind of situation it is as well to have someone in the background on call in case of difficulties.

The women illustrated are mostly self-taught. This reflects the fact that in the early stages of a new development the standard routes for acquiring skills – training courses – are not normally open to us. This is no longer so in

*Frankenstein

computing and there are now ways of getting preliminary training, although it is often hard to get something that fits the bill exactly. Mary (Chapter 8) is an example of someone who was able to make an instant movement in the direction in which she wished to go, once she had had some professional training. Sixteen weeks is not a lot, but it is a good start in a subject much of which can be self-taught, or learned by experience once the basic groundwork has been done.

Money is the other important variable. Computing equipment is expensive and there is no skirting the problem. Kate Jennings (Chapter 7) needed a quality printer as well as a business computer. The printer, a Qume Sprint 9, cost more than the computer at £1795 with a hopper added later at £595. Now she has enough business to warrant a fast draft printer as well, but starting up involved some kind of financing. Both she and I were fortunate in having parents able to help us. Nora's brother assisted her with her computer and expensive accounting software. Marjorie (Chapter 9) had saved the money in preparation for retirement. Drusilla (Chapter 7) built up from relatively modest beginnings, paying her way with her earnings. Even so, the original capital outlay was several hundred pounds and for many people this would be impossible. If you see it as an investment in yourself and your future, you have to decide what you think you are worth and perhaps what you could persuade someone else, like a bank manager, that you are worth. If you already have a professional skill, like accounting, the chances are that he will welcome you with open arms and press you to borrow more than you feel happy to take. If you have no skills and are starting up at random, as I did, then money from that source may be hard to come by. There are opportunities to rent or lease equipment; this, like renting a flat, can get you something for which you cannot put the money down and is usually more expensive in the long run. However, it does protect you against obsolescence.

Most of the examples given are of professional women reborn after child-rearing. Kate Jennings had few educational qualifications and left school at sixteen and so is perhaps nearest to the 'average' woman. Anyone with some clerical or secretarial experience, particularly if it included word processing, who could get hold of a computer, a word-processing package and a spreadsheet of the 'calc' family could find plenty of work to do from home: not simply text preparation, but also organizing things like conferences, clubs and ancillary services of many kinds. The advent of Prestel and Micronet, combined with the ease with which computers can now be linked to the telephone system, must open up new fields and new services. Even such traditional computer tasks as data preparation can be done from home and transferred to larger machines by telephone link or disk exchange.

There seem to be qualities in many women that are a positive aid to making a contribution to the world of computing. You must have a starting point, an idea or something to motivate you. Once you have started there are often difficulties, but these can be overcome by dogged determination rather than by exceptional brainpower. Although support of some kind may be needed – moral, technical or financial – there is no reason why Atalanta should not continue to win races despite pausing to pick up the golden apple of motherhood.

Part III

# Practical Measures

*Chapter 11*

# Learning the Lingo

### The language of computing

People always hate the jargon and unfamiliar terms that come into use alongside any new development and it is probably true to say that the words used in computing are more dreadful and harder to derive than in most professions. They illustrate quite often the – what seem to outsiders – illogical associations and patterns of thought of people who work with computers. Many of the words used can be explained by tangential or laboriously worked references to familiar terms. I have dealt with 'bootstrap' in Chapter 7. Then there is 'bug'. A bug is an error of a kind that is not a straight fault like incorrect arithmetic or a program that does not do what it says it does, but rather an obscure error in logic which causes unexpected consequences and which it is hard to trace. There is a connection here with the virus kind of bug, but it is not a direct one. (There is a story, perhaps apocryphal, which explains the derivation of 'bug' in quite a different way: the development of a program was held up for some time before it was discovered that a large moth was lurking in the machinery upsetting its functioning.) 'Menu', 'memory', 'port', 'strings', 'real numbers' – these are all terms which make sense once you know their use, but which do not correspond exactly with the everyday meaning of the words. Terms like 'byte', 'EPROM' and 'printed circuit board' are somehow easier to learn because there are no fuzzy parallels to confuse one.

Whether you like it or not, you cannot enter computing without learning what some of the words mean, even if you choose not to use them yourself. You could not purchase appropriate equipment without mastering the concept of a 'kilobyte' or 'K', although the precise meaning is irrelevant. I shall therefore go through some of the essential terms, roughly in the order in which you might expect to meet them rather than in alphabetical order, as it is more useful to group words that are likely to be found in association. Before itemizing and explaining individual words I shall give a very brief description of a modern small computer.

The external visible attributes of a computer comprise a screen on which information – either words, numbers or drawings – may be displayed (output); a keyboard on to which letters and commands can be typed by human beings as a method of passing information or instructions to the computer (input); a small box which contains the central core of the computer – the processor and the memory and other bits to make them work – and frequently also the disk drives, although these are sometimes cased separately. These parts make up the essential elements of the machine, without which it would be difficult for ordinary people to use.

Screens and keyboards used to be regarded as separate 'peripheral' equipment, as they are not in fact vital to the working of the computer part but are merely important as a means of access to the user. Nowadays a business or professional computer would be expected to have both. A home computer usually does not include the screen as it uses a home television set for reasons of economy. The display has less definition and the letters are harder to read on a television; this is quite all right for games or intermittent serious use, but not suitable for office use or any kind of regular work. Similarly, a home computer can manage quite well without a printer and often uses a cassette tape recorder instead of floppy disks for backup storage, but both printer and disks are needed in an office environment. Printers are still regarded as peripheral and have to be costed out separately.

**Memory.** One of the first things to consider when thinking about a computer is the amount of memory that will be required. Memory is the means by which the computer holds on to information either on a temporary basis while it is live or on a permanent basis when the power is switched off. There are several different kinds of memory to cope with the different requirements of long- and short-term remembering.

Units of measurement for memory are **kilobytes,** referred to as **K** for short. A **byte,** 1024 of which make up a kilobyte, is not necessarily of fixed length but when used in this way is assumed to be a standard size. Without going into complex and unnecessary details, it suffices to know that a letter of the alphabet takes up one byte of space, a whole number smaller than 32,767 takes up two bytes and a number with figures after the decimal point takes up four bytes. Thus, if you have a machine with 1K (1024 bytes, or 1000 for ready reckoning) of memory space, then you can store approximately 1000 letters, or 150 words, 500 integers (whole numbers) and 250 real numbers (with figures after the decimal point). Even this is optimistic, as there are bound to be what we call 'system overheads'. This explains why people get worked up about whether a machine is 1K, 16K, 48K, 64K (the smallest size for a business computer) or 256K. But even then there are problems, because there are various types of memory, so what have you actually got with your 64K?

**RAM** is one type of memory. The letters stand for Random Access Memory, which may not get you much further at first but contains the essence of an idea. Random Access Memory is like a loose-leaf folder. First, you can reach into any part of it and pick out a sheet to read; second, you can write to any new page in it and, third, you can keep re-arranging the order. There is a limit to the size, as there might be to a folder that came supplied with a certain number of pages which could be wiped clean and written over, but which had a total area of usable space that could not be exceeded, at least without an 'upgrade' or 'add-on'. The RAM area of a computer is memory that is provided on a set of chips and is available to the user to enter facts on to, or to read back existing information from. Areas can be wiped clean and re-used; any place in it can be identified by an address; information can be retrieved more speedily than from disk or tape-storage spaces, or backup storage; and it is usually volatile.

**Volatile** is a word used to describe the kind of memory that is wiped clean, or emptied, when power is switched off. This applies to the immediate (or Random) access memory of most traditional computers, but the newer portable computers are using CMOS chips and this makes them miraculously able to preserve data when switched off. New vistas of possibilities are immediately opened up and when technology is able to provide this facility cheaply and on a large scale, the usefulness, and more important the ease of use, of computers will be much improved.

**ROM** refers to Read Only Memory. This also comes on chips, built into the machine, but it is not volatile. Whereas RAM is like a blank-paper area for you to enter information, ROM is more like a printed book. You can read from it but cannot write to it yourself. It can therefore be programmed in a different way which fixes the instructions or data – code of one kind or another – permanently in place. Thus it is safe from user error, corruption or any ordinary form of loss. There are several varieties of ROM, some of which can be re-programmed (EPROM = Erasable Programmable Read Only Memory), but only by a special method not available to the average user.

**Backup** memory or storage usually comes on medium, which requires a peripheral device such as a disk or a tape. It is known as 'backup' because it is separate from the computer and should be untouched by local disasters. When you use the contents of a disk you actually pull a copy into RAM and work on it there, only going back to disk to save or back up the data. So if the power fails or the computer screws up in some way the copy on the disk is safe. A floppy disk is most commonly found on micros, but Winchester, or hard, disks are becoming more common. They hold much more data and are faster and more reliable.

This should now begin to indicate why the amount of K per item can be important. A RAM of much less than 64K on a business machine means that it will be difficult to run certain programs, whereas on a home computer 48K is regarded as a large amount of RAM. The point illustrated is that the activities appropriate to various types of machine are also different and likely to have different requirements for memory, both type and amount. The capacity of disks is not usually much smaller than 100K and can go up to 40 **megabytes,** which is 40,000K or 40 million bytes of space. This is obviously colossal, but you would need more for preparing the Oxford dictionaries, an encyclo-paedia or some kinds of medical records. Large disks hold more than cassette tapes. Tapes on microcomputers work too slowly to be regarded as cost-effective in business or professional work but are often quite satisfactory for home use (beware of the new fudging of distinctions). The Sinclair microdrives, for instance, sound like disk drives but they are not. By a clever method, they use tape in a way that resembles the activity of a disk drive, but they are neither as fast nor as capacious as disks.

So, having described a computer and indicated that the amount of memory that you will need depends very considerably on the use that you have in mind for the computer, let us now consider the terms **software** and **hardware.** The things that I have described so far are mostly items of hardware. Hardware is the actual physical components, such as the circuit board with the chips on, the box, screen and keyboard and the peripherals like a printer and disk drives or tape recorder. Memory, though a soft concept in ordinary life, has to be provided on physically tangible objects on computers, as we are really referring to containers for information stored or consigned to memory by the computer. There may be memory cells in the human brain, but we do not think of our own memory as being physical in the same way.

Software is much closer in concept to the product of the human brain. It is the knowledge of how to behave, how to tackle a certain problem, which the computer has to get from somewhere before it can go into action and stop being a heap of nuts and bolts – or transistors and integrated circuits or whatever is the computer equivalent. This knowledge comes to us in various ways: it is often the product of long training through childhood, or it may be the result of education, training on a particular course or just watching other people. The computer can only respond to instructions, but these can often be complex enough, and the response quick enough, to give the impression that it knows things in the same intuitive way that we do. In fact, it is always responding to coded instructions which, if properly written, will take it through the steps of reasoning, or retrieving information from its physical store of remembered items (stored because some previous software has instructed it to record the information). These can be accessed and read, and altered if necessary, by people who have learned the codes. Such people are programmers. Programmers write software, and software is simply a list of instructions to the computer which, if properly thought out and encoded, enable the computer to go through steps exactly as you would if you were carrying out some activity by reading the instructions step by step from a book.

Software divides into three broad categories. The first is language software – software for programming with, the tools of the trade. The other two are the products of programmers working with language software. One is systems software and that is necessary to get the various bits of the computer and its peripherals to work in harmony. Before a program stored on a disk can be used it must be loaded from disk into RAM. The systems software has to see that this operation is carried out smoothly. Systems software may divide into smaller categories. OS typically means Operating System. DOS means Disk Operating System. BIOS means Basic Input Output System – i.e. how the user successfully communicates with, puts information in and gets it out of, the system. Language software or extra bits of system can be loaded into RAM (for immediate access) off the disk, but let us for the moment suppose that we need an applications program. This is the third, and for the user the most obviously important, type of software, although it cannot be written or be run without the other two.

An **application** is a subject or activity to which the computer can usefully be applied as a tool. Company accounts are often better done on a computer; accounting packages are an item of application software. Word processing, database management (computerized filing), statistics, graphic design – all these are the appropriate targets for applications software. The programs, whether provided on disk, tape, in ROM or whatever is the latest medium, have first to be called up, and when this has been done it is the software that gives the computer its current identity. It may temporarily change from being a vehicle for Pacman and Lunar Crabs to being a French teacher, an aid to statistical calculations or a telephone link to Prestel or the company mainframe computer in Hong Kong.

**Communications** is another umbrella term often met in computing. When human beings communicate it is most often by means of speech, using their mouths for output and ears for input, or by letter, using words on paper and the eyes and brain to decode the message. The first way is not currently available to computers; nor is the second, but it does provide a sort of analogy. If it is important to transfer information from the computer to another piece of equipment, then the problem of communicating must be overcome. Even a printer is not part of the computer, and must have first the instructions and then the data sent to it before it can print. In order to be able to do this there must be a physical opening – a 'port' – which is rather like an electric socket in the wall. By connecting the printer to the port in the computer, using a wire as with an electrical appliance, we are in a position to start communicating. Now the software takes over and sends a message. As with human telegraphic or postal communication, there must be a passing device, connected at both ends, and an agent who puts the message in motion, either by dropping it in the post box or speaking it down the telephone line. On a computer you need a **port,** an **interface** (a matching connection which may be a simple bit of wire, but can be much more complex) and communications software. Only then can computers communicate either with each other or with other devices.

It is very often desirable to send messages around in this way. There may be a central accounting system which collects local data; electronic mail systems rely entirely on communications of this kind; you may have written a program that would be useful to a friend who has a different kind of computer; you may be one of the growing body of people who use the telephone to connect to such systems as Prestel or Micronet 800.

The speed at which messages can be sent is indicated by the **Baud rate.** This can range from 75 (7.5 characters per second) to 19200 (1920 characters per second) on average. The rate for sending data along the ordinary telephone network is 300 Baud and for direct communication this would be considered slow. Most computers should go up to at least 4800 and business computers to at least 9600. The higher the number, the faster the rate.

One of the most important ports, which should ideally be supplied as standard on every machine, is known as **RS232.** Another is called **Centronics,** and is often used to connect printers. Ports are sometimes referred to as I/O ports. This means Input and Output for putting in and taking out information.

**Networking** is a form of communication that allows computers to be in touch not merely with a central computer, or 'file-server', but also with each other. The lines of communication are not many computers talking to one, but many to many. This can be very useful in a large company.

**Printers** come in various shapes and sizes with odd names to confuse the beginner. The most widely used are probably those called **dot matrix** printers. These print by a method that produces little dots set close together to form the shape of each letter. This method has the advantage that the dots can be reformed by software commands to make different shapes of letter and thus varied typefaces. It has always been a cheaper method than any other, but in the early days it got a bad name because the dots were widely spaced and unattractive. That is no longer true, but daisy wheel or some kind of impact printing is still regarded as necessary for what is called 'letter-quality' work. This may change eventually as the quality of dot matrix print gets better and better. Dot matrix printers can produce graphic output more easily than other types of printer and they are much faster. The fastest office type of daisy wheel printer, costing over £1500, prints about sixty characters per second. Few dot matrix printers are slower than seventy characters per second. For £450 you can buy one that prints at 160 characters per second (cps) and around £2000 would purchase one that prints at from 200 to 400 cps.

**Daisy wheel** printers use a mechanism more like that of a typewriter. Instead of stalks coming out and hitting the page, as in an old-fashioned typewriter, the letters are bunched together on a flower-like head on a single stalk (hence the name). The head moves round and hits the page when it reaches the right place. The timing is crucial and for this reason it is quite difficult to provide the software that allows it to do proportional spacing (see below). Both types of printer are noisy, but the advantage of using a computer is that you do not have to print at the same time as you type. You can store the text silently as you write it and, when you go off to lunch, set the noisy printer in motion. For people who need to print constantly there are other solutions, such as acoustic hoods.

**Proportional spacing.** On a printed page the letters are spaced proportionally to the size of the letter. For instance, the letter 'i' needs less room than the letter 'm'. If a software package like a word processor is to control a printer so that the wheel spins irregular distances in proportion to the size of the letter, then it must be programmed with the exact spacing. The wheel has to be told to spin for as long as it takes to hit the next letter and this movement has to be calculated. For this reason, although most daisy wheel and some dot matrix printers provide for proportional spacing, it has not always been implemented by the writers of the word-processing packages. There are so many makes of printer, all requiring special software, that it could become a full-time occupation. If the package does implement the proportional spacing of the printer, the effect is astonishingly different and more attractive than the same-space-per-letter effect that is to be seen on most computer print outs.

The particular piece of work that is thought of as a separate item is generally referred to as a **file** in programming and systems language but as a **document** in word processing. A letter is a document, and so is a chapter of a book if it is held as a single item. If it is held in two parts it will be two documents. A computer program will normally be referred to as a file, and this term also applies to the working matter of a database management program. Company records held on a database will be held in files. Each file is clearly identifiable by its contents, which will be items of information separated into individual **records.** The information in these records can be broken down further into **fields.** For instance, details of each person constitute records. The individual pieces of information – name, age, sex, rate of pay, etc. – are known as 'fields' or, if we slip occasionally into research language, variables. It is worth remembering these terms because early conversations with suppliers are often made a nightmare by the assumption that you understand them.

Different sizes of computer are grouped into broad categories and named by type. A **mainframe computer** is a giant computer, typically costing hundreds of thousands of pounds. A **minicomputer** costs tens of thousands and probably services a medium-sized business rather than something the size of a university. A **microcomputer** costs under £10,000 and the category is broken down into sub-groups. These are: desk-top or business/personal computer with a full set of peripherals such as screen, which is not a TV screen but a monitor or terminal, keyboard, disk drives and not less than 64K of RAM; home computer, which does not usually have a screen since a TV set can be used, and which normally has from 1 to 48K and tape cassette for backup; and portable, which is small enough to carry in a briefcase, is battery operated, has integral screen and sometimes printer and cassette drive as well, smaller amounts of RAM and ROM, and should be able to communicate (link up to) a larger computer if it is to be useful.

Armed with these terms you should be able to fight your way through the jungle of computer talk. There are hundreds of others, and you will need to build up your vocabulary as you go. The words given above form a tourist vocabulary which will enable you to make a start.

*Chapter 12*

# Suitable Equipment

It is difficult to recommend equipment in an industry moving as fast as the computer industry. Sir Clive Sinclair has brought a new machine out each year for four years, and each one has had something new and special to offer. However, what is the poor customer to do if no one will risk giving advice? I shall therefore discuss equipment, and even name names, but the items discussed must be regarded as typical of a category and not necessarily the latest and best by the time you read this. If there has been a real quantum leap (*pace* Sir Clive) in the interim, then there is nothing that will cover it. There is much talk about generations, but I think that there will be some generational sub-divisions before we get to the true Fifth Generation – the expected quantum leap.

It is absolutely essential to grasp the difference between a personal computer of the type known as 'desk-top' or 'business', and a home computer. Having said that, I have then to admit immediately that the boundaries are becoming somewhat blurred and it is possible to get a machine that is good for both purposes, and probably for development and programming work as well. However, there are not many such, and caution is the name of the game. The differences lie in the amount of memory available, the availability of disk drives, the kind of screen, the operating system and the ability to interface to other equipment. All these seriously affect what you can expect to be able to do with the computer that you choose.

The issue is further confused by the recent arrival of portable computers, which, while they are in most ways tools for professional rather than home use, nonetheless lack many of the facilities that are necessary for a serious business or professional micro. I will look at them separately after I have outlined the main differences between home and business computers.

## Memory

### RAM or immediate memory

Let us look first at the crude differences. A home computer will not in general need as much memory as a business computer. It will be running games and programming languages and some software which may sound similar to that found on larger machines, such as word-processing, accounts and database packages, but which will usually be a cut-down or less elaborate version. This is often perfectly satisfactory for what one wants to do at home and usually easier to use than its more sophisticated counterparts, since by leaving out the more complicated options it can be more simply presented. The BBC machine, for instance, has a first-rate word-processing package which costs £40 and uses a tape cassette, thus avoiding the need for expensive disk drives. Word-processing packages on disk-based machines usually start at nearer £200 and you will probably only ever use about 10 per cent of the potential for everyday work. If, however, you are thinking of setting up a word-processing business like Kate Jennings (Chapter 7) you will simply be wasting your money if you buy a home-computer type of package as you will need something more sophisticated once you get off the ground. What does 'more sophisticated' mean? In word processing it means all the extra options like different character pitches, super- and sub-scripts, varying line heights, the ability to insert page headings and footings, varying page numbers, conditional page breaks; the ability to move columns from tables, print in columns, overprint a line, pause to change a daisy wheel, use a mailing system, run another program from within the word processor and so on and so forth. For a database management system there would be a similar list of necessities.

### Backup memory

*Quantity.* The quantity of backup memory that is required is likely to be greater for the purpose of storing data and files produced by a database management system (which might be your library references or your company personnel details), an accounts package or whatever, for a business than for a home-based application. An ordinary cassette tape holds varying amounts, according to its size, and may take between 50 and 250 kilobytes of information. Few tapes allow data to be accessed in the random way that is possible with disk drives, however, and so the maximum usable size of an individual file will usually be limited by the size of the RAM in the machine. Thus, although you may have decent storage space, you still cannot have large individual files and this is often crucial to a serious piece of work. Data can be found quickly and loaded in and out of RAM memory in chunks from a single large file on a disk. Files can be megabytes large – 5 or 6 million characters – for a large database on a hard disk. New technology and clever programming is beginning to provide similar facilities on tapes, but this is the exception rather than the rule and, in any case, tapes are still slow and not recommended where time is money. The new Sinclair QL has 'microdrives' which are tape drives, not disk drives, with more than tape-recorder-like facilities. A system called RAX has been developed for the Epson HX-20. RAX stands for Random Access Cassette and allows the accessing of data in a non-sequential way from tape cassette. Other methods will probably be devised, but serious work is still usually better done with disk drives on a desk-top or business machine. Machines are currently coming on to the market with sufficient backup memory in either RAM or bubble memory to open up new ideas, but for the moment it is better to stay with conventional computing terms and avoid confusion. I will say a little more about the new developments under the heading of *Portable computer*.

*Speed of access to backup memory.* Disk drives are superior to tape recorders if speed is important. A file that takes a few seconds to load from a disk can take up to fifteen or twenty minutes from tape, and even small ones take minutes rather than seconds. Home computers occasionally sport disk drives, but are more likely to be tape based. Unfortunately, disk drives are still very expensive and are one of the features of business machines that make it difficult for manufacturers to bring prices below a certain point. Perhaps this should be the next target for technological improvement.

### Availability of disk drives

Some machines can be used first of all with tape recorders and later be 'upgraded' to use disk drives. This is what Drusilla Clavert (Chapter 7) did when building up her system for indexing. It is essential for serious business use to have the option of disk drives, for reasons given in the preceding paragraph.

### Type of screen

A computer screen can be one of three things. The cheapest is a television screen, used as a medium of output. This is the solution for most home users, but the letters and symbols are not produced with as much clarity as on either of the other two methods. The output is good enough for occasional use, but definitely a source of eye strain and unsatisfactory for regular use, and certainly would cause a downing of tools in a word-processing pool. The next option is known as a 'monitor'; it is a screen designed to take computer output and is much clearer and of better quality than a television screen. The cost of a monitor ranges from £70 to about £200, and some of those included as part of the integrated design of a desk-top computer are of excellent quality. The third type of screen is known as a terminal and has traditionally been used as the local work station of a larger and more expensive computer, such as a mini or mainframe or a dedicated word processor (a computer which performs word processing only, rather than general applications). The quality of these is better than anything but the best monitors, and the keyboard is usually part of the design and often of better quality than those on micros. A terminal would be useful only with a computer that did not have keyboard and monitor already included as an integral part of the design, and this is becoming less common.

Some computers allow you the choice of using a television or a monitor. These tend to be the machines whose designers are aiming to bridge the gap between home and business computing, and with such a machine you can start with your television screen and later upgrade to a monitor, if your starting budget is tight.

## The operating system

The meaning of the words 'operating system' is discussed in Chapter 11. Computers can have either an operating system that is peculiar to them or one that is general to a genus of computer, but not usually both. Home computers more often have individual operating systems, but if you are buying a business system it is important to buy a computer with a general operating system unless there is a very good reason for doing otherwise. This is because software packages – and software is what determines the usefulness or otherwise of your computer – will run only on the operating systems for which they have been written. A single machine operating system, therefore, is bound to be limited in the amount of software available for it. Even if you choose a general system you will find that there are several different such operating systems, and that you are still limited to software that will run on machines of the same family. However, most of the really popular packages have been re-written for other general systems, but not so often for the individual ones as there is not enough money to be made out of so doing.

It should be said that, although this is the correctly received doctrine in the professional computer world, the general public tends to ignore it. For business use this is a mistake, but for a purpose that is individual to you and likely to be run as a stand-alone operation it may not matter.

### Linking to other equipment

A home computer may have various interfaces which enable it to use joysticks for games or to run a standard printer or a piece of robotic equipment. A business computer must have a proper set of interfaces to allow it to run serial or parallel printers, disk drives or plotters; to allow it to communicate with (pass information to and from) other computers; and, increasingly important, to allow the 'networking' of several computers. It may be desirable to have sound output, and some home computers provide better facilities for this than business machines.

The essential ports are RS232 and Centronics parallel. These are a minimum provision, and the ability to control disk drives is also a must. This involves systems software as well as hardware. Real time clocks and sound generation facilities are coming to be considered important, and generally, the more potential a machine has, the better it will be able to respond to changing demands.

## Portable computers

Portable computers are relatively new and defy previous forms of categorization. The Osborne was probably the first computer to claim portability, though it is now described as 'trans-portable'. The term 'transportable' in this context refers to a computer that can be carried with relative ease. It is just light enough, but not so light that you would willingly carry it for long distances and, although it needs electricity, it can be transported from home to office and vice-versa. It needs either to pack everything required except a printer into a single unit or else use a television screen as a display unit.

A truly portable machine is now required to run without access to mains electricity and therefore to be able to run on batteries. It must have a screen built into the main unit and ideally should have printer and cassette drive either included in the single unit or provided as small battery-operated additions. This means that the computer can be used on the move – in a train, a factory or workshop, in the desert or as an aid to the disabled in classrooms and so forth. Some such computers are actually pocket-sized and several makes are no larger than an A4 piece of paper. With a nice shoulder bag or briefcase they make the ideal travelling companion.

The memory available in these portable computers, though getting larger every year, does not measure up to my criterion for a business or serious computer, and yet they are serious. This is because the uses are different. Software exists to allow them to be used as rather primitive word processors. The output can be sent direct to a printer if you have no other machine, but if you have a desk-top computer, then the text prepared on the portable can be 'down-loaded' to the larger computer for final editing and printing. This means that work can be done away from home, or in the garden or on a cheaper second machine which can use the more sophisticated facilities of the first when necessary. Kate Jennings bought a portable computer (Epson HX-20) as a second machine when she began to get enough work to take in partners. Later she bought a transportable (Wren Executive) as work expanded more and ate into her children's long holiday periods and the family's country weekends. Although such a computer allows work to invade every corner of your life, it does also allow you to go away with the family when you still have a pressing load of unfinished work.

## Machines currently on the market in each category

\* denotes home computer (requires VDU or TV and often a tape recorder as well; limited memory)

\*\* denotes desk-top (integral screen and disk drives; can run full complement of peripherals and has enough memory for standard software – 64K for 8 bit systems and 128K for 16 bit)

[\*\*] denotes hybrid (more often home, but has facilities that make it possible to use for professional activities; often these machines are particularly useful in education)

∧ denotes portable (battery operated; 'can be carried for a mile without difficulty by a child of ten')

∧\* denotes transportable (requires power but compact and light enough to be carried without difficulty in a carrying case)

| | |
|---|---|
| \* | Sinclair Spectrum |
| \* | Oric |
| \* | Dragon |
| \* | Commodore Vic |
| \* | Commodore 64 |
| \* | Electron |

| | |
|---|---|
| \*\* | IBM PC |
| \*\*∧\* | Wren Executive |
| \*\* | Epson QX10 |
| \*\* | Sirius |
| \*\* | Apricot |
| \*\* | Apple II, Lisa and Macintosh |
| \*\* | Future |
| \*\* | DEC Rainbow |
| \*\* | Commodore – various |
| \*\* | ICL |

| | |
|---|---|
| [\*\*] | Sinclair QL |
| [\*\*] | BBC |
| [\*\*] | Newbrain |

| | |
|---|---|
| ∧ | Epson HX-20 |
| ∧ | Epson PX-8 |
| ∧ | NEC 8201 |
| ∧ | Sharp – various |
| ∧ | Tandy 100 |
| ∧ | Casio |

- ^ * Osborne
- ^ * Kaypro
- ^ * Commodore
- ^ * Wren Executive System
- ^ * Pied Piper

The best-known dot matrix printers are those made by Epson. There is a range of good low-cost ones (£300-£450) and also the new LQ (letter quality) dot matrix which produces typeface to rival a daisy wheel at half the price (£1100) and twice the speed.

Other printers include the OKI range, Toshiba, NEC, Centronics and, most expensive but excellent heavy-duty, fast machines, the Anadex range.

Daisy wheel printers at the bottom of the range – slow but good quality – include the Juki and the Brother (around £400).

Expensive and faster daisy wheel printers include the Ricoh Flowriter, the Diablo range and the Qume (£850-£2000).

## Software

*Word processors*

WordStar, Perfect Writer, Peachtext for CPM machines

Word wise for BBC computer

Provided with Sinclair QL

Various for other home computers

Volkswriter and the Word for IBM

Intext for Epson HX-20

Provided with NEC and Tandy portables

*Databases*

Cardbox for CP/M and MSDOS – excellent card-index program

Delta for CP/M and MSDOS – quite powerful and 'user friendly'

dBASE II for CP/M and MSDOS. One of the most powerful – takes a little learning but has all the necessary facilities, such as maths, as well as string information handling

Superfile for CP/M and MSDOS – many special features and worth investigating, especially for anything involving long text records.

Home computers have a range of smaller programs. The flexibility and performance of these is bound to be limited compared with those written for disk-operating machines, but will use the basic mechanisms and concepts. It is necessary to check fairly carefully what each program does. *

*Spreadsheets*

Supercalc for CP/M and MSDOS

Visicalc for Apple and Pet systems

Perfect Calc for CP/M and PCDOS (IBM)

Many others, including Multiplan, Micromodeller, Lotus 1-2-3, etc.

Home machines will have their own versions. Check out the size of spreadsheet allowed and the possibilities of linking or consolidating files

*Programming languages*

All languages (including BASIC, Pascal, FORTRAN, COBOL, C language, LISP, FORTH, subsets of Ada and many others) should be available for CP/M computers and increasingly for MSDOS and CP/M86 (16 bit)

Home computers usually have BASIC and machine code only

Portable computers usually have BASIC and machine code and sometimes one or two more

*Accounts*

On CP/M and MSDOS computers the best-known accounting packages are Pulsar, TABS and Peachtree. These are the market leaders, and though they are not the most specialized or necessarily the best, they are the safest to go for.

On home computers you will have to find packages individual to the make of computer. It is particularly important to investigate what these do in accounting terms because, though they may be quite well written in programming terms, they may not satisfy the requirements of accountants or the Inland Revenue. You need to know a little about accounting to ascertain their suitability. Otherwise, you will have to take a risk and be prepared to have wasted your money at least once before you find the right package.

Think about your application, present and future. Buy for the future if you can, but remember that the learning part is as important as the rest and you will get further faster by starting with something, no matter what, rather than with nothing. Be prepared to make a mistake and pay for it since you will almost certainly be able to do so with the increased earnings and improved position in the job market that will result from getting to grips with computers. If possible, buy the best; if not, get started somehow.

---

*For an outline of what can be expected from a database see Database Primer, R. Deakin, Century, 1983

*Chapter 13*

# Getting Started: Training

Getting started in anything is the worst problem, and it is especially difficult in something as unfamiliar and mystique-ridden as computing. There are, as should by now be plain, so many different trades and skills within computing that it is difficult to give advice on how to start. For some a training course in a particular skill will seem the best. Most universities and polytechnics now run a variety of courses at various times of day, full time or part time. Get the information and try to see whether anything sounds useful or attractive. It is easy to spend a lot of time learning things that are slightly tangential to what you really need to know, but you have to start somewhere. If you look in the professional computer papers – mostly distributed free within the trade, so you need to find a computer professional in order to see one – you will see advertisements for courses and also for firms providing training for future employees. These are usually aimed at the younger age group. Even the TOPS courses specify an age range of nineteen–thirty, or on the business computing course, twenty-five–thirty-five, which is depressing for women who are returning to work after a stiffish bout of child-rearing, as they may well be over thirty-five and feeling fit and ready for work.

The Manpower Services Commission is working hard to provide a network of courses throughout the country and the number and range of these seems to increase daily. Booklets have been prepared and should be available at your local library, giving details of the courses available. The booklet for

London courses, entitled *Computer Training Opportunities in London* has the following table of contents:

> What is TOPS?
> Can I apply?
> How do I apply?
> What happens then?
> Do I get help with the cost of training?
> A job after training?
> What courses are available?
> Data Entry/Preparation
> Computer Operator
> Computer Programmer
> Systems Analyst
> Maintenance Engineer
> Data Communications Technician
> Micro Electronics Technician
> Computer Sales

Under the heading of 'Can I Apply?' the booklet says: 'TOPS courses are open to men and women who are at least nineteen years old and have been away from full-time education for a *total* of more than two years.' Some of the courses, when advertised, place an age limit, but looking through the booklet, although an age range is often stated, the words used are 'applicants should *preferably* (or, sometimes, *usually*) be aged between nineteen and thirty-five', so it should be possible to fight your way on to one if you are older. It is an issue that should perhaps be taken up by the Equal Opportunities Commission, since in career terms a woman of forty-five is equal to a man of thirty-five. She has had a break in her career and has a longer expectation of life and, in these days of early retirement, an equal number of working years ahead of her. Moreover, women returning to work after child-rearing often have all the dedication and determination of a young man at the start of his career.

These TOPS courses are slightly biased towards learning to program rather than simply to use computers, but that is in any case a valuable grounding. They cover such useful topics as accounts programming, computer programming for business applications, microcomputing and office technology, business systems analysis, micro systems sales and marketing.

The desperate need for people to take up computing is such that a half-page advertisement appeared in the London *Standard** headed:

*6 April 1984

# UNEMPLOYED BUT INTERESTED

# IN BREAKING INTO

# COMPUTERS OR ELECTRONICS?

### (and get paid while you train for a new career)

A new London Computer and Electronics School has been set up in Hammersmith and is being sponsored by the Manpower Services Commission. There will be other such schemes around the country and in order to find out about local possibilities you should go to the local library and write to the Manpower Services Commission for details. The address is: *The Manpower Services Commission, Training Services Division, Moorfoot, Sheffield.*

Mary (Chapter 8) did the TOPS course in business systems analysis and Christine's (Chapter 9) course in Word Processing at the polytechnic was sponsored by the Manpower Services Commission. Another fruitful source of training opportunities is the local polytechnics and institutes of further education. A booklet, also obtained from the local library, entitled *Fresh Start – a Guide to Training Opportunities* by the Equal Opportunities Commission, and which describes itself as 'A guide for women on how and where to train for a new job', gives an excellent list of useful addresses, including those of the National Institute of Adult Education, the Open University, and the Women's Research and Resources Centre.

Local Education Authorities organize and fund many of the evening classes that are available all over the country. Some local evening institutes have courses in first steps BASIC programming which are designed for parents and children learning together. In *Floodlight,* the catalogue of courses provided throughout London by the Inner London Education Authority, there are three pages of courses on various aspects of computing. In practice, lists like this can be a little daunting and many of the courses geared to more nervous individuals produce special leaflets using more encouraging layouts and vocabulary. It was one of these which led Christine to her first course, and it is worth a look in your local library to see if you can find anything similar there. Remember that the best leaflets are produced at the beginning of a course, which is usually September or January, but tend to disappear in the intervening months, when you will have to rely on more formally compiled indexes and catalogues. Christine had been given a typed list of courses on computer and micro technology in her area and it featured twelve colleges, polytechnics or evening institutes, and a total of forty-one courses, ranging from evening courses in A-level computer science, through part-time day courses in word processing to introductory evening courses 'including BBC linked'.

Most libraries will also be able to lend you a copy of *Never Too Late To*

*Learn,* a complete guide to adult education by Judith Bell and Gordon Rodence. This gives the addresses of Local Education Authorities, district offices of the Manpower Services Commission Training Service Division and the National Extension College (18 Brooklands Avenue, Cambridge), which is another good source of home-study opportunities and a place which early concerned itself with computing. Another book readily available in libraries is *'Second Chances 198—',* which is an annual guide to adult education training opportunities. The 1983 edition has useful chapters on studying with children, women, and details of various courses on computing, such as the City and Guilds course, the BBC course and so forth.

The City and Guilds part-time courses include C&G 746 – Basic Certificate in Computer Programming – and C&G 747 – Certificate in Computer Programming and Information Technology. These are professional training courses which can be taken on a full-time basis. There are also courses for the B/TEC National Certificate and National Diploma in Computer Studies. These courses can often be found in Colleges of Further Education.

The message is really that you must look around for what is available in your own locality. Probable sources of information are the local library, the Local Education Authority and the Manpower Services Commission. Probable locations for courses are the local higher and further educational establishments, the Open University, local groups (especially women's groups) and, finally, privately run courses. These vary from excellent to very poor and are always expensive, so use them only as a last resort. They, like the others, will probably advertise in local papers.

If there are no courses available to attract you, or if you are turned down by everyone as too old, then you will have to find ways of teaching yourself. I hope that the examples that I have given in Chapters 7-9, almost all of whom are entirely self-taught, encourage the idea that it is possible to learn enough about using computers to earn a good living and have an interesting job, often self-employed, without going on a course. Most of the individuals concerned would have taken a course had there been one, and it is preferable to have help, but not essential. Learning out of books, as they mostly did, is no longer the only way. If you buy a standard micro you can now also buy self-teaching courses on tape and disk for many of the interesting uses of micros, including the operating systems and other such traditional obstacles.

Finance is a stumbling block as great or greater than lack of know-how. If you cannot afford to buy a machine outright, there are agencies which finance the leasing of machines and also organizations which arrange to rent systems. Such firms advertise regularly in the computer papers. Like renting a house, this is more expensive in the long run, but it is a way of getting started in the absence of cash. Banks also now understand about computers and it seems for many people to be easier to borrow money from the bank to buy a computer than for any other purpose.

Let us suppose now that you have raised the money but had no formal training, and you have decided to go ahead and buy a computer. You have considered very carefully the different categories of microcomputer and you have been around to several computer outlets or stores, probably within reasonable reach of your home. You have asked advice and taken note, not merely of the content of the advice, but also the manner of its delivery. You have, unless your neighbourhood is particularly barren of such people, found someone whom you judge would be helpful and understanding after the sale as well as before. Perhaps it is even possible to purchase training from your source of supply, both in basic starting procedure and in word processing or programming or whatever you have decided to start with.

All the decisions have been made. Now it is time to take the computer home. If you have not arranged to have the computer installed in your home (and the margins on computer sales are so slim that this may not be a free service) you may have problems, depending on how good at such things you are. If in any doubt, ask the supplier to show you (perhaps using his demonstration model rather than your neatly boxed up product) exactly what to do and which bits connect (and which way round) with each other. It is very easy and obvious once you know, but it can be traumatic until you do.

Once the computer is home and connected it is really up to you and the manuals. These are usually many in number, inches thick and hard to understand. Sorting out the instructions and the documentation is the hardest part of learning to use a computer. There is so much of it, all necessary at some point but often not in the first instance, and it is usually badly written. The standards of documentation are improving and may soon reach a reasonable state. It is not malice but fact that the task of writing about so many and such complex matters in a simple, compact way defeats most writers. One firm of software writers analysed all their telephone calls and found that 80 per cent of the calls asking for help were the consequence of bad documentation. As they themselves wrote the manuals for their programs, they set about earnestly to improve them. You may need to get the help of your supplier when it comes to unravelling the documentation and finding out which of the many manuals is the important one to start with; this is something else which might be best sorted out before you leave the premises to take your prize home.

Once you have started using the computer there will inevitably be some problems, but if the equipment is in good order, these should all be surmountable. The only really important thing to remember, right from the start, is to make copies of all software. The manuals will tell you to make working copies of your master disks which contain programs, but they usually omit to tell you to make copies of all your work as well. You should save every half hour or so, once you have reached the stage where your work is worth saving, and make backup copies on to a second disk or tape at least every day that you work. If you have a disk system, care of the disks is of the utmost importance. Keep them upright, in their covers, away from heat, and do not put greasy finger marks on them.

I am straying now into the details of using the computer, which is another whole book. My intention was to get you started, and I find it difficult now to call a halt and abandon you to your fate. The best teaching is probably self teaching, as you learn more thoroughly that way, but you will need help from time to time, so be grateful for all the tips that are offered to you by enthusiastic computer friends along the way.

## Chapter 14

# Conclusion

I can only conclude by trying to hammer home the points at which we have been looking in the preceding chapters: the arrival of computing at the micro level and its penetration into nearly all spheres of work is an unparalleled opportunity for women; it is all out there and up for grabs; it is not impossibly difficult, although it requires persistence; there are some training opportunities, but it is possible to manage without; there are opportunities for old women, young women, practical women, intellectual women, women of only moderate ability; in almost every walk of life, but especially in many traditionally female fields of work like teaching, nursing, office work of all kinds; and it is more susceptible to being carried out at or organized from home, and on a part-time basis, than almost any other job except journalism or some kind of creative art, and, unlike them, you do not have to have a special gift to be successful.

I started this book with the intention of showing that there was no evidence that women could not be as good as men at information technology and its related skills. The belief was partly based on my conviction that there are no inherent superiorities to be found between different classes in society or different races in the world, and that there was, therefore, unlikely to be a basic inferiority in women. This kind of argument has to be susceptible to the converse, and so I have been a little embarrassed to find indicators here and there that women, far from being inferior, may be superior. Educational journalists have told me, and remained stout under further questioning, that what they observe in schools in both the USA and the UK is boys sitting square in front of the computer with the girls edged physically to one side. If they watch closely and listen to what is being said, they observe time and time again that the girls are making the correct suggestions for solving the problem in hand; their suggestions are brushed aside by the boys, who then take three attempts to get it right. The teachers (both male and female) usually seem to be unaware of this; the boys themselves are certainly unaware of it and have a clear sense of superiority. Expressed in more cautious terms, these comments have not been contradicted by those of Her Majesty's Inspectors of Schools with whom I have had discussion.

I cannot cast aside my belief that there is no innate superiority in either sex, but can perhaps advance the 'different contributions' theory and allow a tentative hypothesis that women have a special contribution to make to the development of computing and the use of information technology. Thus, there are two main conclusions to be drawn: first, that computing offers women a special chance and, second, that men ignore it at their peril in this world where commercial competition is between companies and national groups rather than between individuals or the sexes.

# Notes on the Text

1. General Household Survey 1981
2. *Sex-Related Differences in Cognitive Functional Developmental Issues,* ed. M.A. Wittig & A. Petersen, Academic Press Inc, 1979
3. *Men and Women,* John Nicholson, Oxford University Press, 1984
4. *New Scientist*
5. *Men and Women,* John Nicholson, Oxford University Press, 1984
6. *Faster than Thought,* ed. B.V. Bowden, Pitman, 1953
7. *Information Technology in Schools,* Equal Opportunities Commission
8. *The Rights and Wrongs of Women,* ed. Mitchell & Oakley, Penguin, 1976
9. *Men and Women,* John Nicholson, Oxford University Press, 1984
10. *The Rights and Wrongs of Women, ed. Mitchell & Oakley, Penguin, 1976*
11. 'Women in Computing: meeting the challenges in an automated industry', Russ Adams, *Interface Age,* December 1983

# Glossary

**Acoustic coupler:** a modem which connects to the telephone without the need for special wiring. The telephone handset fits into 'cups' on the modem and connection is made acoustically rather than electrically. (See **Modem**.)

**Address (actual, absolute** or **relative):** the position in which items of information are stored inside the computer's immediate memory. These can be referenced or identified on the memory map by an address. This can be actual or absolute (i.e. the exact number of the location) or relative (e.g. a displacement from another item, whose address may vary but is known to the program at a given moment, +1).

**Algorithm:** a method for 'doing' a task, or devising a procedure to follow in order to solve a problem. Algorithm design, sometimes as a flowchart, means deciding what to do in an organized, step-by-step way before you do it.

**Alphanumeric:** letters and numbers mixed.

**Analogue:** the conversion of a signal into a different signal which is 'analogous' to it, e.g. the conversion of digital (i.e. computer) information into electrical signals. Compared to digital signals, analogue information has an infinite number of possible levels, not just on/off. An 'A to D' converter means a device which converts analogue to digital information, and a 'Da to A' system reverses this translation.

**Analyst (systems):** a person who determines how best a computer can be used to solve a problem. This is done by breaking the problem down into separate and simple steps – analysing it into component parts. After that the decisions about programming and appropriate equipment and methods can be made.

**ANSI:** American National Standards Institute. Equivalent to our BSI.

**Applications:** these are the things that you can actually do with the help of a computer – the problems to which you can apply it. Applications programs are written to be applied in a particular context: word processing, accountancy, etc.

**Array:** a table or matrix of information. A one-dimensional array is a single line with some columns made up of separate items of information. A two-dimensional array has rows (or lines) and columns. The rows and columns are accessed by names which stand for the number of the row or column.

**ASCII:** American Standard Code for Information Interchange. A standard code using binary numbers to represent characters in a computer. The binary numbers can be translated into hex or decimal numbers. Letters of the alphabet, for instance, in ASCII decimal are entered as: 65 (A), 66 (B), . . . 90 (Z). A question mark is 63 while a comma is 44. This also means that alphabetical ordering can be done numerically by the computer.

**Assembly language:** a computer language where the instructions represent single machine operations. The instructions are short, usually three or four letter words, like XCHG for 'exchange contents of specified registers', or JNZ for 'jump if not zero'. These are easier to remember than numbers, but only involve a single-step conversion into the number code to which the machine can respond.

**Assembler:** a program to convert assembly language into binary codes which can be interpreted by the computer.

**Backup:** make spare copies of everything in case of an error. *Always* use backup copies of important programs and keep the master copy safe so that you cannot ruin it.

**Bar code:** a method of coding numbers into thick and thin lines so that they can be read directly into a computer by means of an electronic wand (used on library tickets/books, supermarket products, etc.).

**Baud:** 1 bit/sec (by some definitions) used to measure data signalling rates. It is used to measure the speed at which data is transmitted over any serial link – e.g. RS232 or modems. A number of fixed standard speeds are normally used, such as 300,1200,9600,19200 Baud. Generally a byte or character will need two or three extra bits added to it before it is sent. Thus at about 10 bits per character, 300 Baud will equal approximately 30 characters.

**Benchmark:** a standard program to do a particular known activity. These programs can then be run on different systems as a 'benchtest' to see which one does it quickest, best, most efficiently, etc.

**Binary:** a numeric representation with base 2.

**Bios:** a part of the CP/M operating system (*see below*) which is used to transfer data between the processor and the VDU, disks, etc.

**Bit:** the smallest piece of information in a computer. The word comes from contracting binary digits. A bit is therefore either 0 or 1. The processor in a microcomputer is often described, according to the number of bits of information that it can handle simultaneously, as 8 bit or 16 bit. One day there will be 32 bit micros.

**Boolean:** a form of algebra used to simplify logical equations.

**Bootstrap** (or **boot**): a short program held in ROM, which is used to load a larger and more powerful monitor program into a computer when it is turned on first.

**Bubble memory:** a form of memory where bits of data are stored in minute magnetized bubbles which can be recognized as north or south poles by an electronic detection circuit.

**Bug:** an inherent design error in either hardware or software. (See *also* **Fault**.)

**Bus:** a circuit (or collection of wires) which is the central circuit for carrying signals around a computer.

**Byte:** a group of bits (usually 8 in microcomputers). A made-up word. An obscure derivative of bit.

**Cassette:** same as a music cassette. Stores information as sounds.

**Character set:** all the letters, figures, symbols and punctuation marks available in a particular computer.

**Code:** as a noun it means a computer program; as a verb it means to write a computer program.

**Command:** an instruction to the computer which gets immediate response, like RUN, PRINT, END, EDIT, or TRACE.

**Compatible:** one of the most important words, unless you want an ivory-tower existence. Indicates that software, and sometimes hardware, can be exchanged between systems.

**Compiler:** a program which converts instructions from a computer language into machine operations.

**Console:** often refers to the VDU. It is the input and output part of the computer as seen from the user's point of view.

**Constant:** a value that does not change throughout the life of some process or program.

**Control character:** a character that causes some control function to be initiated on a peripheral device, e.g. control J, which tells the printer to move down one line.

**Co-ordinates:** same as the mathematical use of the word with xy axes. A useful way of thinking about the screen if you are designing a complicated display, or an array if you are trying to work out a particular value or location.

**CP/M:** control program for microcomputers. The best-known and most widely compatible operating system. Developed by Digital Research Inc.

**CPU:** central processing unit – the part of a computer that obeys the instructions of a program.

**Crash:** when a program loses control of the computer and ceases to work. A system failure.

**Cursor:** a (sometimes flashing) blob or line which indicates the point on the screen at which the next character will appear. The character may be typed by you, or it may be coming over from memory and being sent by the system to the screen.

**Cursor addressing:** the software that sends the cursor back and forth to places on the screen which would not normally be the next expected. Used a lot in packages and games which are enhanced by fancy screen displays.

**CUTS:** Computer User's Tape System. Standard cassette interface. Also known as Kansas City.

**Data:** information sent from one digital device to another. Often used to mean the information or numbers that you ask the computer to process using the particular program that you specify.

**Database:** refers usually to a set of programs which make it easy to handle data in different ways. A substitute for a filing system, so that you can put in any information, cross-reference it, alter, delete and add to it, get it out in various different forms specified by you, etc. Loosely applied in microcomputing to refer to rather more limited systems of data management.

**Dedicated:** limited to one task. For instance, the controller in a washing machine is not suitable for calculating a mortgage repayment, whereas a (general-purpose) computer is. A word-processing machine is really a computer that only does word processing, whereas a word-processor package can be loaded into an undedicated computer which acquires that function for the duration.

**Density:** disks come in double or single density. This indicates how closely or densely the data is packed on to them.

**Digital:** information in digits (discrete numbers) as opposed to analogue (continuous) form.

**Disk:** like a cross between a record and a cassette tape. It is a flat disk, usually made of plastic or metal coated with a magnetic material on to which data can be recorded for later retrieval.

**Disk drive:** an electro-mechanical device used to write to and read from disks.

**DOS:** Disk Operating System

**Dot Matrix:** a printer that forms letters out of visibly distinct dots.

**Edit:** to alter information which is already in the computer. An 'editor' (program) facilitates this.

**Enter:** to put information into a computer.

**EPROM:** Erasable Programmable Read Only Memory. A chip that can be programmed to hold a semi-permanent program which can then be erased and replaced by a new program.

**Expansion:** or expandibility. Like compatibility – be sure you have it.

**Fault:** a fault develops in hardware which has previously been working satisfactorily.

**Field:** a file which is a collection of data will probably be a set of records – e.g. name, address, age, sex, income details for 100 clients. Each item is a field. Each collection of items is a record. Each collection of records is a data file.

**File:** a program or collection of data that is kept, usually in external store like a disk. Temporary files last the duration of the particular piece of processing only.

**Floppy** or **flexible disk:** a disk made out of a thin film of mylar (a type of plastic).

**Format:** a word used a lot in computing. It means layout, or organization of space to take certain items. Disks have to be formatted to take data in a way in which it can easily be found again by the operating system. Screens are formatted for easy reading of display information. FORTRAN requires format statements for reading in and writing out data.

**Formfeed:** automatically push the next page through the printer, leaving a bottom-of-the-last-page, top-of-the-next-page margin.

**Graphics:** visual aid output. Pictorial display on screen or paper.

**Hang up:** this means that the system has given up the ghost. Usually it is because you have asked it to sit in a programming loop doing nothing. It therefore 'hangs up' rather as someone on the end of a telephone might do if the conversation became too much for them.

**Hard copy:** a permanent form of computer output (results) normally obtained from a printer.

**Hard disk:** a disk made on solid material such as aluminium. Hard disks have a much greater storage capacity than floppies.

**Hardware:** the part of the computer that hurts you if you kick it; the equipment and physical devices.

**Hex:** hexadecimal.

**High level language:** language which is nearer to ordinary language and is several removes from the binary system. Includes: BASIC – Beginner's Allpurpose Symbolic Instruction Code; APL – A Programming Language; FORTRAN – FORmula TRANslation; ALGOL – ALGOrithmic Language; COBOL – COmmon Business Oriented Language; Pascal; Ada; PL/1 – Programming Language/1; LISP – LISt Processing language; STOIC – STack Oriented Interactive Compiler.

**Input:** the information put into a computer program.

**Integer:** a whole number such as 7, 8 or 115, 980.

**Interface:** a matching connection between two components such as a computer and a printer.

**Interpreter:** a software program that translates or interprets the programmer's instructions into machine operations. It does this line by line as it meets them. This is in contrast to a compiler, which translates the program as a whole before it can be run.

**I/O:** Input and Output. The means by which a computer talks and listens to the outside world – e.g. keyboard, printer, VDU.

**Justify:** to align the left and right margins of a printed document, as in a newspaper column.

**K:** a short way of referring to kilobyte. 1K, or a kilobyte, is 1024 bytes, not, as might be expected, 1000 bytes. This is because it is actually two to the power of ten, not ten to the power of three, which is how a kilogram or a kilometre is calculated.

**Key:** as in keyboard. Also the field or item of a record by which you identify or sort each record – e.g. in a telephone directory the records which contain name, address and telephone number are sorted using the name key.

**Kilobyte:** 1024 bytes of memory.

**Language (computer):** a defined set of words and rules of grammer which can be used to write instructions for a computer to follow (a program).

**LCD:** Liquid Crystal Display. Used in place of an ordinary VDU or screen on some portable computers, such as the Epson HX-20.

**Linefeed:** moves the display on the screen up by one line, with or without a carriage return which 'ends' the line.

**Low level language:** *see* **Assembly language** – the language nearest to the ground of the computer.

**Machine code:** instructions to the machine reduced to their final binary form so that the circuitry can treat them as switches or gates. All higher level codes have to be translated into this by the compiler, interpreter or whatever.

**Mainframe:** a large, fast, expensive computer. Wordsize is usually greater than 32 bits.

**Maintain:** program maintenance. A euphemism for repairing faults in a computer program. Long programs are always delivered with bugs in them and program maintenance is largely the process of repairing these faults as they show themselves. Other operations may include extending or adapting the program.

**Medium, media:** tape, disk, etc., on which information is stored.

**Megabyte:** a million bytes.

**Megahertz:** one million cycles per second. The speed at which a computer operates.

**Memory:** the part of the computer which is used to store programs and data.

**Microcomputer:** a small computer, usually 8 bit words, fairly slow, costing from £50 to £20,000. Usually suitable for one user, or at the expensive end, 5 to 10 users.

**Minicomputer:** a smaller computer, often 16 bit words, costing around £20,000 and usually capable of supporting 10 to 40 users.

**Modelling:** simulating the effect of a series of events (using a computer).

**Modem:** a MODulator/DEModulator. A device that converts computer signals into sounds which can be transmitted via the telephone lines. A modem has to be connected between the computer and the telephone line before data can be transferred and the modem, usually a small box of electronics, converts the outgoing data into sounds and converts incoming data from sounds into digital information the computer can understand.

**MS–DOS:** Microsoft Disk Operating System, available on some 16-bit (*see* **Bit**) machines like the IBM, Sirius and the Apricot.

**Networking:** linking several computers together in order to share a group of common peripherals.

**Octal:** a number system using base 8 – i.e. digits 0 to 7.

**Online, offline:** online means linked up to the computer and offline (or local) means temporarily disconnected.

**Operating system:** the program that handles communication between the user and the computer.

**Output:** the results generated by a computer program.

**Package:** a program, or more often a set of linked programs, which carry out a useful general function, and can therefore be used by different people. This makes the programs cheaper than custom-built software, and in the long run should provide tried and tested ways of doing things.

**Parallel:** as opposed to serial. This refers to the bits in a byte or word travelling in parallel along a number of wires, instead of one after another, serially, along one wire.

**Parameter, parameter driven:** a parameter is a value which is fed into a program or subroutine. Within the program the value is assigned to a variable. Thus 'parameter driven' means a program that is affected by values which you, the user, put in. This might be a payroll, where you enter the relevant information about tax codes, and thus can alter it yourself if the rules change without having to return to the software house to have the program rewritten or brought up to date.

**Parity:** an extra bit which is added to a byte or word of information and used to check that the information is correct.

**Patch:** a small alteration to a program.

**Peripherals:** extra devices used with the computer – e.g. printer, disk drive, etc.

**Port:** a communications channel to a computer. Every peripheral would be connected to one or more ports.

**Power supply:** necessary to make the mains electricity suitable for use by the computer.

**Prestel:** British Telecom's Teletext service (a large public database).

**Processor:** same as the CPU. The action part of the computer. Processor chips are many and various. Machine code and operating systems are processor dependent to a very large extent, because the processor is the vital doing element – the verb of the computer.

**Printed circuit board (PCB):** a board with a circuit (lines of wires) set or printed on to it. Chips are then plugged in and link up with the various bits of the circuit to complete the design.

**Printer:** peripheral device for producing print out on paper. There are many different types and a very wide price range. The types include: line printers, daisy wheel, thermographic, electrosensitive, electrostatic, impact, inkjet and matrix printers. Needs studying separately before you make a choice.

**Program:** a set of instructions to the computer sufficient to produce some desired result. There must therefore be a beginning, some consequence and an end.

**PROM:** Programmable Read Only Memory.

**RAM:** Random Access Memory. You can write to it as well as read from it, and it is the memory that is available to the user as blank paper.

**Read:** retrieve from memory or store.

**Real number:** a number which may have a decimal fractional part – e.g. 5.4. Not a discrete number, which is called an integer.

**Reboot:** *see* Boot.

**Record:** a list of data items linked to one source – e.g. an employee record is all the information about a single employee. It will be made up of various fields – name, address, age, occupation, length of service, overtime rate, etc.

**Resolution:** the degree of accuracy to which something can be represented or displayed – especially graphically.

**R/O:** Read Only. Often given as an error by the operating system if you try to write on a disk that is write protected, or Read Only.

**ROM:** Read Only Memory. You can get items of information or program instructions from it but not write any on to it. It is set into a chip, is fast to access and cannot be destroyed by user mistakes – as a book is not destroyed even when we misunderstand what is written in it.

**RS232:** an international signalling standard. This is a protocol which defines a serial interface between two pieces of communications equipment – e.g. a computer and a terminal.

**Save:** store on some kind of external memory like disk or tape.

**Screen format:** the height and width of a VDU screen (measured in character positions) – e.g. 24 x 40 is 24 lines of 40 characters. Common formats are 16 x 64 and 24 x 80, which is the width but not height of an A4 piece of paper.

**Scroll:** move the display up and off the screen to make room for more at the bottom.

**Select:** term used to indicate that data is being picked out by various criteria. Same as cross-tabulation – you 'select' by various keys.

**Serial:** one after the other – e.g. data items stored on cassette tape.

**Software:** programs that control the computer's activity without switches or movement. The brain that we give to the computer.

**Sort:** to arrange a list of items according to a given criterion or 'key'.

**Spreadsheet:** a way of handling information, usually numbers, similar to that used on a sheet of paper which has been ruled out into rows and columns for accounts or financial forecasts. Formulae, headings and figures can be put in and manipulated. Changes can be made and instant "What if" situations tried out on the screen as the computer recalculates the whole spreadsheet at great speed and re-displays the changes immediately.

**Store:** there are various kinds. Immediate access store is the memory in the central part of the system. Backing store is tape or disk, etc.

**String:** a sequence of characters.

**Support:** help and information given to a user by a manufacturer or software house after a computer or software package has been purchased.

**Syntax:** as in ordinary use – the correct grammar of a language. You have to be especially punctilious with computer languages.

**System:** (i) collection of hardware and software items that go together to make a computer, (ii) as in systems analysis. (*See* **Analyst.**)

**Terminal:** a piece of equipment that incorporates a VDU and a keyboard. It is used to enter and display information to and from the computer. Often wrongly called a VDU.

**Update:** to update a file is to alter or enter new items. An update is a new version of a program, which is provided to a user who already has the original version.

**Value:** what the variable has in it. The value in a variable which symbolizes names will be a string of letters forming a name. The value in a variable which symbolizes an integer (number) will be a particular number.

**Variable:** like x or y in algebra, this can be anything. Almost like a container into which you can put a value and then manipulate it. A substitute or representation.

**VDU:** Visual Display Unit. A piece of equipment which displays information on a screen like a TV set. The information can be text graphs or line drawings.

**Volatile:** disappears (or empties, if it is memory) when the power is turned off.

**Winchester:** a hard disk used as a backing store for information. Called 'Winchesters' after the code name given to the IBM project that developed them in the 1960s, these disks are capable of storing far more information than floppy disks – between 10 and 50 times more.

**Word processor:** a computer program used to prepare letters, documents, etc.

**Write:** write to or cause to be recorded in memory or store.

# Index

accounts 36, 56, 61, 76, 122
acoustic coupler 133
acoustic hood 113
Ada (programming language) 122
Ada, Countess of Lovelace 26
adult education 125
advertising 31, 33, 36
analysis 18, 26
analysts 47, 48
Analytical Engine 26
Apple computer 74, 76, 97, 120
application 56
applications, software 111
Apricot 120

Babbage, Charles 26
BASIC 92, 96, 122
baud rate 112
BBC: computer 30, 62, 116, 120;
    Radiovision series 29
Bernstein, Danielle 31
Bird's Eye Walls 46
Blackstone, Tessa 29, 34
Bloomfield, Christine 95
book keeping 36, 96
British Aerospace 46
British Computer Society 46
British Petroleum 90
Brixton, Information Technology
    Centre 23
bubble, memory 117
Byron, Lord 26
byte 108

C language 122

Calvert, Drusilla 79
Cardbox 121
Centronics interface 112, 118
character pitch 116
chemistry 23, 90
child-minding schemes 38
children: dependent 16, 48; school-
    aged 16
City and Guilds 126
club, micro-users' 39
CMOS chips 109
COBOL 92, 122
commerce departments 36
Commodore 62, 64, 120; Vic 120
Commodore computers 120, 121
communicate, ability to 16, 17, 18,
    19, 26
communications 111
computer: business 108; desk-top
    114, 115; home 114, 115;
    mainframe 114; micro 114; mini
    114; personal 115; portable 114,
    116, 118; transportable 118
computer clubs 30
Computer Services Association 24
computer studies 22, 23, 28, 30, 32,
    35
Computer User's Yearbook 93
Computertown UK 38
Computing 23
Confederation of British Industries
    46
Cooper, Professor 34
CP/M 58, 60, 90, 121, 122
Croydon: London Borough of 28;

report 30; schools 29, 33

daisy wheel 82, 113
data capture, remote 55
database 77, 88, 91; examples of
    121
dBASE II 83, 121
DEC Rainbow 120
decimal, tabs 81
Delta 121
discrimination, pay 42
disk 109; care of 127; Winchester or
    hard 110, 117
disk drive 79, 108, 110, 115, 116
document 82, 113
documentation 18, 127
DOS 98, 111
dot matrix 112
Dragon computer 120

earnings of women, average 43
editing 79
education 17, 33, 34; further 38
educational, literature 28
Electron 120
electronics course 96
EPROM 109
Epson computers 60, 83, 117, 119,
    120
equal opportunities 17, 20, 23
Equal Opportunities Commission 28,
    34, 124
European Social Fund 38
evening institutes 38
expert systems 47

F International 24, 44, 45, 46, 47,
    48, 61
field 113
Fifth Generation 27, 115
file 113, 116
finance 58
*Floodlight* 15

FORTH 122
FORTRAN 122
Forward Trust 46
Franglen, Nora 73
*Frankenstein* 27
Future Technology Systems 120

games 11, 28, 35, 108, 116
Genealogical Association 38
genealogy 97
general public 64
Godwin, William 27
Government Skill Centres 24
graphics 29, 91, 111; high resolution
    28
Gregg, Pauline 41

hardware 110
Haringey Women's Technical
    Training Centre 38, 95
holiday camps 23
home computer 56, 108, 114, 121;
    market 31
hopper, sheet feeder 82

IBM 36
IBM pc 61, 120
ICL 44, 120
indexes, for books 56, 59, 81
indexing program 79
Industrial Revolution 41
industry, cottage 42, 80
Information Technology (IT) 17, 34
Information Technology Centre 23;
    Brixton 23; Southwark 24
Inner London Education Authority
    125
input 108
interface 115, 118
Intext word processor 121
Island Logic 64

jargon 93, 107

Jennings, Kate 80
job satisfaction 42, 43
journalism 18, 69

K 108
Kaypro 121
keyboard 57, 93, 108, 110
kilobyte 108

laboratory 43
Laurie, Peter 35
layout, document 82
leasing, equipment 126
library, public 38, 125
Lisa 120
LISP 122
Local Education Authorities 34
logical, abilities of women 26
LOGO 22
Lotus 1-2-3 122

Macintosh 120
Macrex/Micrex (Indexer) program 60
mailing system 75, 116
MailMerge 83
mainframe 18, 85, 114
management 26, 34, 43, 47, 48
Manpower Services Commission 92,
    123, 126
manuals 127
mathematical: abilities of women 26;
    principles 36
maths 35
megabytes 110, 117
membership lists 56, 61
memory 35, 107, 108, 110, 115,
    116; bubble 117
Menabrea 27
methods, traditional 16
microdrives 110, 117
Micromodeller 122
Micronet 90, 103, 112
Middlesex Polytechnic 96

Milbanke, Annabella 27
Mill, John Stuart 27, 34
Morgan, Augustus de 27
Morgan, Mrs de 27
mothers, working 16
MS-DOS 58, 121
Multiplan 122

National Computing Centre 92
National Extension College 125
National Institute of Adult Education
    125
NEC8201 120
networking 112, 118
Newbrain computer 120
Newell, Mrs Alison 46
newsletters 61
Nicholson, John 34
nurses 36, 55

office work 18, 36
Open University 86, 88, 125, 126
operating system 21, 115, 118
Oric 120
Osborne 120
output 108

paginating 79, 80
Palmer, Mary 92
Pascal 86, 88, 122
Peachtext 58, 121
Peachtree accounts 122
Peachtree office software 84
Perfect Calc 83, 122
Perfect Filer 83
Perfect Speller 83
Perfect Writer 58, 83, 121
*Personal Computer World* 38
physics 23
Pied Piper computer 121
point-of-sale 55
polytechnics 38
*Practical Computing* 31

presentation 28, 32; classroom 36
Prestel 90, 103, 111, 112
printers 108, 112; Anadex 121;
    Brother 58; Centronics 121;
    Diablo 121; Epson 60, 83, 121;
    Juki 121; NEC 121; OKI 121;
    Qume 82, 121; Ricoh Flowriter
    58, 121; Toshiba 121
processor 108
programmers 47, 48, 111
programming 18, 24, 30, 35, 38, 44,
    63, 86, 96, 97, 115, 116;
    languages 122
proportional spacing 82, 113
Pulsar accounts 122

QL: Sinclair 117, 120; Sinclair 62

RAM 109, 116
random access 116
Rank Xerox 44
RAX 117
re-training, opportunity 19; youth 23
real time clock 118
record 113
research 60
Richards, Janet Radcliffe 43
ROM 109
RS232 112, 118

St Paul's Girls' School 30
sales consultant 17, 18, 36, 44, 69,
    89, 91
school 22; comprehensive 22; out of
    23; primary 22
Scott, Gloria 45
screen 108, 110, 115, 117
self-help groups 38
service engineers 78
Sharp computers 120
sheet feeder, hopper 82
Shelley, Mary 27, 102
Shirley, Mrs Steve 45, 46

Sinclair: QL 62, 70, 120; Sir Clive
    115; Spectrum 62, 70, 93, 120;
    ZX81 62, 97
Sirius computer 61, 120
Smith W.H. 69
SNAP, survey package 61
social attitudes 33, 36
social patterns 30, 41, 45
social research 85
social work 17, 36
socialization 29, 30
Society of Genealogists 98
Society of Indexers 39, 79
software 42, 47, 58, 65, 90, 110,
    116; applications 111, language
    111; systems 111
Somerville, Mrs 27
sound output 118
South Glamorgan's Women's
    Workshop 38
spatial concepts 26
Spectrum, Sinclair 62, 70, 93, 120
Spellbinder, word processor 84
spreadsheet, examples of 121
Statistical Package for the Social
    Services 60
statistics 60
status 16, 28, 43
stereotype 22; sex 33; traditional 35
Stewart, Marjorie 97
Study Group for the Use of
    Computers in Survey Analysis 61
Supercalc 84, 122
Superfile 121
Superwriter 58
systems: analysts 47, 92; designers
    47; services 47

tabs, decimal 81
TABS accounts 122
tabulation 81
Tandy portable computer 97, 120
tape-based system 79, 108, 109,

116
teacher 17, 22, 30; guidelines for 35;
  training courses 34
teaching 16, 18, 55; aids 28
technical drawing 23
technological revolution 45
telephone link 43, 103
television 108
Todd, Sarah 90
tool, computer as 32, 36
TOPS 24, 92, 123
training 18, 64, 83, 123
Transam Microsystems Ltd 87
typing 36, 56, 81

VDU 95
verbalization 26
visicalc 77, 122
volatile 109
Volkswriter 121
voluntary organization 38, 56

Wilkinson, Jane 44
Wollstonecraft, Mary 27

Women's Research and Resources
  Centre 125
Word, the 58
word processing 21, 23, 43, 56, 57,
  96, 111, 116
word-processing courses 125
word processor 77, 91; dedicated
  25; examples of 121
WordStar 58, 81, 121
Wordwise 121
work 30; freelance 46; home-based
  15, 19, 43, 46; office 18; part-time
  16, 46, 48; pattern 16, 45, 48;
  return to 16; semi-skilled 16; shift
  16; traditional pattern of women's
  15, 19, 29
workforce, women in 24
working mothers 16
Wren Executive System 58, 60, 61,
  90, 119, 120, 121

XBASIC 79

ZX81, Sinclair 97